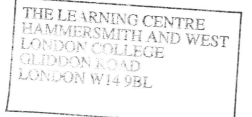

Best practice partnering in social housing development

M. Jones

School of Construction Economics, Management and Engineering,
Faculty of the Built Environment
University of the West of England
Bristol

V. O'Brien

Western Housing Consultancy Services
Bristol

ThomasTelford

Published by Thomas Telford Publishing, Thomas Telford Ltd, 1 Heron Quay, London E14 4JD.
URL: http://www.thomastelford.com

Distributors for Thomas Telford books are
USA: ASCE Press, 1801 Alexander Bell Drive, Reston, VA 20191-4400, USA
Japan: Maruzen Co. Ltd, Book Department, 3–10 Nihonbashi 2-chome, Chuo-ku, Tokyo 103
Australia: DA Books and Journals, 648 Whitehorse Road, Mitcham 3132, Victoria

First published 2003

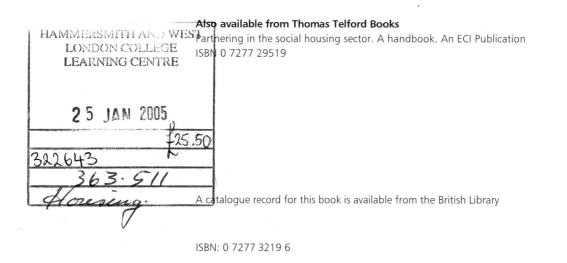

Also available from Thomas Telford Books
Partnering in the social housing sector. A handbook. An ECI Publication
ISBN 0 7277 29519

A catalogue record for this book is available from the British Library

ISBN: 0 7277 3219 6

Typeset by Helius, Brighton and Rochester
Printed and bound in Great Britain by Hobbs The Printers, Hampshire

Contents

Preface

Partnering aims to break down the traditional barriers between the parties in the development process through the building of more collaborative and synergistic customer–supplier relationships. It was given considerable impetus by the publication of the Latham Report in 1994, by Sir John Egan's Construction Task Force with the publication of its report *Rethinking Construction* in 1998, and reinforced in the report *Accelerating Change* published in 2002.

These seminal reports acknowledged that the world is changing significantly and we are entering a new and challenging business era. What worked in the past will not necessarily work in the future, and organisations, like society at large, are having to change in unprecedented and unanticipated ways in order to remain competitive and survive. More and more organisations are responding to these challenges by simultaneously making themselves more customer- and supplier-facing. This involves not only internal changes to their own organisation but also developing closer and more collaborative relationships with their suppliers and customers in the supply chain. These latter changes are taking place owing to a growing climate of opinion that more collaborative ways of working have considerable advantages over the more traditional adversarial relationships.

Within the social housing sector there are strong pressures on registered social landlords to find new ways to create and deliver greater value to their tenants. The Housing Corporation is actively promoting the use of partnering for scheme developments 'provided it is implemented in a well-planned way that clearly demonstrates value for money and addresses the issue of probity'. Consequently, a number of registered social landlords have been experimenting with partnering as a means to continuously improve the development process in ways that demonstrably add more value for their tenants and provide mutual competitive advantage for the whole supply chain.

Best Practice in Social Housing Development aims to provide practitioners in registered social landlord, consultant and contracting organisations with a framework and tools for working more collaboratively. It presents a robust approach for adopting, implementing and sustaining partnering aimed at continuously improving performance and increasing mutual competitive advantage. Using its seven-element model, registered social landlords can decide whether to partner and the form it should take before moving on to develop the most appropriate supply chain relationships, structure and processes. The text aims to be strategic in its perspective, conceptual in the way it explains the nature of partnering, practical in the coverage of the key ideas and issues involved, and realistic in terms of the scope of partnering possible given the substantial difficulties involved and the barriers to overcome.

Although it is aimed primarily at development practitioners in registered social landlord organisations, it will also be a useful tool for consultants and contractors and their supply systems as they position themselves individually and collectively to adopt more customer- and supplier-facing, collaborative and synergistic approaches to new scheme developments for registered social landlords. As no single text can possibly cover all aspects of partnering within the complexity of the social housing sector, the report ends with an extensive biography and list of useful websites where further information and advice can be found.

Glossary

Action research. A combined form of research and consultancy in which practitioners receive help with problem-solving whilst the researcher/consultant is able to contribute the knowledge gained in the process to the academic community.

Asset specificity. The degree to which a supplier's assets are made available to a specific customer.

Benchmarking. A management tool which allows firms, project teams and supply chains to rigorously examine and compare business practices with the 'best in class', aimed at creating and sustaining excellence.

Best value. Introduced by the DETR on 1 April 2000, the concept requires continuous improvement in terms of efficiency, effectiveness and economy.

Big picture mapping. A visual approach designed to display at a high level a major part or whole of the supply chain.

Champion. A key member of staff who is committed to driving the partnering process forward.

Charter. The document mutually agreed and signed by all the parties and which establishes the principles and objectives of the partnering arrangement. It should incorporate a statement of purpose, a mission statement, and the objectives of the partnering arrangement, sometimes known as the agreement.

Cluster. A group of suppliers – designers, specialist and trade subcontractors and suppliers of materials and components – who take responsibility for the design and delivery of a major element of a building or scheme whilst working to drive out waste, reduce costs and add value.

Continuous improvement. A fundamental basis of total quality management, it consists of measuring key quality and other process indices and taking continuous actions to improve them.

Core processes. Those central processes that directly deliver results against targets.

Critical success factors. Those key external or internal elements that a business needs to focus on for success, such as market growth or employee involvement.

Culture. The system of meanings and ways of working which are shared by members of a human grouping and which defines what is good or bad, right and wrong and what are the appropriate ways for members of that grouping to think and behave. See also *organisational culture*.

Framework. An arrangement that allows a series of projects to be encompassed by a single general contract with provision for each project to be subject to separate specific terms.

Guaranteed maximum price (GMP). A guaranteed maximum price offered by a contractor as a ceiling in a cost-recoverable situation.

Key business processes. Patterns of interconnected value-adding relationships designed to meet business goals and objectives, or the main cross-functional activities required in a business for success.

Mapping. The use of appropriate tools and techniques to analyse the current situation in any process.

Mediation. A facilitated process of reaching mutually agreed outcomes.

Models. Analytical schemes which simplify reality by selecting certain phenomena and suggesting certain relationships between them.

Necessary non-value-adding. Non-value-adding activities which are necessary under the present operating system and procedures. They are likely to be difficult to remove in the short term but may be possible to eliminate in the medium term by changing processes or technologies.

Non-value-adding. Those activities within a company, project or supply chain that do not directly contribute to satisfying end consumers' requirements. It is useful to think of these as activities which consumers would not be happy to pay for.

Open book. A payment system based on actual recorded cost with total access for audit.

Organisational culture. A set of ideas, values, attitudes, norms, procedures and artifacts characteristically associated with an organisation.

Organisational structure. This includes all those relatively stable aspects or regularities in behaviour within an organisation whether they are formally or 'officially' sanctioned or not.

Pareto analysis. Sometimes referred to as the 80:20 rule. It recognises that in many business situations a small number of factors account for a large proportion of events. For example, in terms of quality, 80% of defects might be attributable to 20% of causes.

Partnering. An arrangement to direct the resources of separate organisations for mutual benefit.

Policy deployment. A strategic decision-making tool that focuses resources on the critical initiatives necessary to accomplish the critical success factors of the firm or partnership. The term usually also encompasses the cascading of this by key business processes together with the control, measurement and feedback of results.

Power. The capacity of any group or individual to affect the outcome of any situation in such a way that access is achieved to whatever resources are scarce and valued within that group.

Project-specific partnering. Relates to a specific project for which mutual objectives are established and the principles and ways of working involved are restricted to the specified project only.

Registered social landlord (RSL). A landlord of properties offered for rent on an economic basis. Includes both housing associations and local authorities.

Risk management. The identification, analysis and assessment of risk and the implementation of a risk management strategy.

Stakeholder panel. A group of people who have an interest in and give effect to a specific scheme development.

Steering group. A group of people appointed to give effect to a strategy or policy such as partnering.

Strategic partnering. Takes the concept of partnering beyond that associated with project-specific partnering to incorporate the consideration of longer-term issues over a period of time or number of projects.

Supply chain. A network of connected and interdependent organisations mutually and cooperatively working together to control, manage and improve the flow of materials and information between suppliers and end users.

Supply chain management. The management of upstream and downstream relationships with suppliers and customers to deliver superior customer value at less cost to the supply chain as a whole.

Target costing. An approach to the development of new products aimed at reducing whole-life costs while ensuring quality, reliability and other end user requirements within a specified cost envelope. Target costing combines a market-driven attitude combined with a disciplined effort to involve the whole supply chain in developing products that offer the best achievable balance between whole-life cost and functionality.

Task force. See *steering group*.

Total quality management (TQM). An approach to the production of goods and services in which employees at all levels focus on 'satisfying customers', use statistics and other techniques to monitor their work, and seek continuous improvement in the processes used and the quality of what is produced.

Value adding. Those activities within a company, project or supply chain that directly contribute to satisfying end customers, or those activities consumers would be happy to pay for.

Value analysis. The value techniques that are carried out following the completion of a scheme.

Value engineering. The term used to describe value techniques that are adopted during the detailed design and construction stages when completed designs or elements of the design are available for study.

Value management. The term used to describe the entire philosophy and range of value techniques. Therefore, value planning, value engineering and value analysis form subsets of value management.

Value planning. Carried out in the early part of schemes prior to the decision to build or at the briefing or outline design stage.

Value stream. The specific activities within a supply chain required to design, order and provide a specific product or service.

Value stream mapping. The process of charting out or visually displaying a value stream so the improvement activity can be effectively planned. See also *mapping*.

Waste. All those activities that occur within a company, project or wider supply chain that do not add to the value of a product or service supplied to a final customer.

Whole-life cost. This includes all capital and running costs associated with the development, implementation and operation of a scheme over its lifetime. Also known as through-life cost and the total cost of ownership.

Whole-life cost model. A cost model in spreadsheet form in which the capital cost appears together with the estimates of maintenance and operation costs throughout the planned life of the scheme. Discount factors are applied to the latter, which are then added to the capital cost to obtain the net present value.

Workshop. An interactive meeting, which is usually facilitated.

Executive summary

There are strong pressures on registered social landlords (RSLs) to adopt partnering and change their supply chain relationships in order to increase both value for their tenants and mutual competitive advantage for the whole supply chain. This requires that RSLs replace short-term, project-by-project relationships with their cost and design consultants, main contractors, specialist and trade subcontractors, and suppliers of materials and components, with long-term, close, and more collaborative relationships.

Partnering in construction is not a unified concept. It takes on a number of different forms including post-award project partnering, project-specific partnering, and strategic partnering. The main reason for the existence of different types of partnering is the diversity of construction's clients and the varying levels of collaboration and integration that are possible in their often quite different supply systems. There is now, however, considerable agreement on a number of partnering's core attributes including the need for:

O   strong and consistent commitment from the client;
O   more open communication;
O   an agreed method for resolving problems;
O   continuous measurable improvement.

Some attributes are, however, more contentious, such as the need for:

O   close and long-term relationships;
O   mutual objectives;
O   the involvement and development of subcontractors;
O   equitable sharing of risks, incentives and rewards;
O   innovation;
O   shared learning;
O   mutual competitive advantage.

The report provides an overview of the Best Practice in Partnering Group (BPiPG) model for an RSL-led approach to developing these new supply chain relationships.

It is seen as particularly relevant in helping RSLs to act on recent procurement guidance from a number of sources including the Office of Government Commerce and the Housing Corporation.

The BPiPG approach acknowledges the pivotal role for RSLs in spearheading this new approach to the reshaping, management and development of supply chains by:

○ ensuring the commitment of their senior management;
○ deciding whether partnering is appropriate for them and their supply chains;
○ deciding the appropriate form of partnering to use, including the closeness, openness and length of the relationships;
○ setting the policy and strategy and disseminating it within their own organisation;
○ having the necessary leverage over their suppliers of construction products and services by providing sufficient volume and continuity of schemes for development;
○ being clear on what constitutes value for their tenants, housing managers and operating departments and communicating it effectively to the supply chain;
○ ensuring that they are prepared internally to partner by having in place the right culture, people and interface structures;
○ being clear on what is expected of suppliers, and agreeing stretching targets for measurable performance improvements;
○ rationalising their supplier bases, restructuring their supply chains and choosing the most appropriate suppliers to deliver the performance improvements needed;
○ building the most appropriate interorganisational relationships;
○ applying pressure:
  – on their suppliers for continuous improvement against housing quality indicators (HQIs), key performance indicators (KPIs) and other mutually agreed performance measures,
  – for the overall coordination and integration of the supply chain,
  – to extend the partnering approach outwards in the process to include local authority enabling officers, and downstream in the process to include specialist and trade subcontractors and the suppliers of materials and components,
  – to ensure the supply chain remains focused on the needs of their tenants, and
  – for the learning and innovation needed to support continuous improvement.

The report has identified a number of benefits that can flow from close, open and more collaborative customer–supplier relationships associated with partnering, including:

○ higher HQI scores;
○ more open communication and the sharing of knowledge;
○ greater certainty in relation to quality, price and programme;
○ more collective learning and sharing of knowledge leading to innovation;
○ more continuity of work for contractors.

The report has also identified the possible dangers associated with this approach to procurement, including:

○ complacency and 'cosy' relationships leading to a loss of competitiveness;
○ overdependency on fewer suppliers and customers;
○ reconciling the different values, aims and objectives of the organisations involved;
○ the possible loss of access to new technologies and management approaches.

The report has also identified some of the barriers to the adoption of these new relationships. The most significant of these is the difficulty many RSLs have in providing sufficient volume and continuity of scheme developments (given the degree of external intervention through complex funding regimes, shortages of sites, and protracted planning processes) to effect meaningful changes in individual and organisational behaviour, interface structures, and ways of working within their supply chains. This is a particular problem for those RSLs with small and/or irregular building programmes as they are unlikely to have the necessary leverage over their consultants and contractors to effect any meaningful change. It may, therefore, be necessary for some restructuring of the social housing sector and its flow of funds so that fewer RSLs have sufficient development programmes and resources to adopt long-term relationships in strategic partnerships or alliances. The Housing Corporation is examining this issue with the publication of its paper *Partnering through the ADP*. As an alternative approach, main contractors could play a larger leadership role in the sector by developing long-term and close relationships with their suppliers, coordinating and integrating inputs and outputs, and presenting these pre-assembled supply chains to RSLs with smaller new-build development programmes.

The report is structured as follows:

○ A discussion of the role of partnering in improving the performance of scheme developments in the social housing sector.
○ A model of partnering practice setting out seven elements of a sustainable approach to partnering in the social housing sector.
○ A series of actions through which these elements can be implemented and sustained.
○ A bibliography and further guidance on adopting, implementing and sustaining partnering in the social housing sector.

Section 1

Introduction

1.1. The Best Practice in Partnering Group and the research project

The Best Practice in Partnering Group (BPiPG) was formed in 1999 to help develop good practice in setting up a partnering approach in the context and culture of the social housing sector in the South and West of England.* This report presents the main findings of the BPiPG's research project, 'Best Practice in Partnering: Development of Guidance on Professional Practice in Partnering for RSLs'. It outlines a registered social landlord (RSL)-led approach to partnering. The BPiPG comprised RSLs, consultants, main contractors, the Construction Industry Training Board, and a researcher from the University of the West of England, Bristol.

The research was funded by an Innovation and Good Practice (IGP) Grant awarded by the Housing Corporation South West Region. In its guidelines the Housing Corporation defines innovation as 'the development, testing and amending of new ideas and proposals which will lead to the generation and promotion of good practice in approaches to housing services and procedures for other organisations to implement', and good practice as 'the collection and collation of existing processes, procedures and practices which are capable of being copied by other organisations'. One of the fundamental aims of the IGP programme is to 'enhance the quality of life of present and future tenants and customers of housing associations and other registered social landlords through improvements to the services they provide'. One of the principal themes of the programme is taking forward the culture of change set out in the Construction Task Force report *Rethinking Construction*.

---

* Three members of the BPiPG, Knightstone Housing Association, Devon and Cornwall Housing Association and the Construction Industry Training Board, had already been working in partnership since 1995 on the 'Employment Opportunities in the Construction of Homes in the South West' (EPOCH) project. This examined how new social housing developments might provide more opportunities for local employment and training in the construction industry.

BPiPG members

Project manager

Vic O'Brien	Knightstone Housing Association (now at Western Housing Consultancy Services)

Researcher

Martyn Jones	School of Construction Economics, Management and Engineering, The University of the West of England, Bristol
Ian Dacre	Symonds Group
Austin Hargreaves	The Construction Industry Training Board
Keith Hodges	Leadbitter Construction
Andrew Lawrie	Bristol Churches Housing Association
Linda Martin	Quattro Design
Jan Randall	Guinness Trust
John Randall	Randall and Simmonds
Phil Spencer	Devon and Cornwall Housing Association
Nigel Sweeting	Turner and Townsend
Steve Thomas	Bovis Homes
Dave Wheeler	The Housing Corporation
David Wood	Midas Homes

1.2. Context

A succession of major studies has highlighted the inefficiencies of traditional methods of procuring and managing construction projects – in particular the fallacy of awarding contracts solely on the basis of lowest price bid only to see the final price of the work increase significantly through contract variations, with the building often completed late. Work by the client bodies since the early 1990s coupled with a major review of construction relationships by Sir Michael Latham in 1994 reiterated the concern of clients about the high level of inefficiency and waste in the industry and called for more integrated project teams and processes. His report, *Constructing the Team*, recommended more standardised contracts, better guidance on best practice and legislative changes to simplify dispute resolution. In 1998, the Egan Report, *Rethinking Construction*, strongly reinforced the concern of clients and urged construction to embrace best practice in supply chain management that had proved its effectiveness in other sectors of the economy such as the automotive industry. It identified five 'drivers' that needed to be in place to secure improvement in construction; four processes that had to be significantly enhanced; and set seven quantified targets, including annual reductions in construction costs and delivery times of 10% and reductions in building defects of 20% a year.

During this period, the government began to reflect these new ideas in the procurement of construction products and services. *Government Construction Procurement Guidance*, a series of guides published by HM Treasury and later the Office of Government Commerce since 1997, states that continuous improvement should be a central part of any procurement option. It goes on to identify the benefits that can flow from strategic partnering arrangements 'because the lessons learnt from one project can be applied to further similar projects through a process of continuous improvement'. This procurement guidance for construction resulted directly from the 1995 Levene Report, *Scrutiny into Construction Procurement by*

Government, and is aimed at central government departments, their agencies and non-departmental public bodies. The main roles of the documents are to remove the threat of criticism from auditors for doing something different from what they have always done; provide documentary support that champions need to persuade skeptics to change their practices; and point people in the right direction without being prescriptive. The guidance documents can be used as they stand or as the basis for in-house guidance and policy.*

The Housing Corporation is also committed to, and actively promoting the use of, partnering in developments 'provided it is implemented in a well-planned way that clearly demonstrates value for money and addresses the issue of probity'. Since 1998, the Corporation's scheme development standards (SDSs) have encouraged partnering as a suitable method of procurement. In its *Guide to the Allocation Process* for the period 1998–1999, the Corporation made clear the government's commitment to implement the principles set out in the Egan Report 'within the next four years'. The Corporation's programme for the implementation of the Egan principles means that by 2003–2004, 100% of the Corporation's Annual Development Programme (ADP) is to be procured as set out in *Rethinking Construction*.

In August 2000 the Housing Corporation published its updated SDSs which again endorsed partnering as a way to 'introduce the cultural and procedural changes necessary to better enable RSLs wishing to embrace the principles contained in the report of the Government's Construction Task Force *Rethinking Construction.* The Corporation also went on to reiterate its commitment to support RSLs in providing the necessary client lead in forming partnerships in the search for quality-based solutions and continuous improvement. Initially, the impetus for partnering and continuous improvement was applied by the Corporation through a set of annual 'proxies' which were designed to take forward the culture of change agenda, referred to as Egan compliance.

In 2001, the report *Modernising Construction* was published by the Controller and Auditor General, and set out how the procurement and delivery of construction projects in the UK can be modernised with benefits to all – the construction industry as well as clients. It identified the need for 'greater concentration on achieving a better construction which meets the needs of the end user at lower trough life costs'. It argued that 'The entire supply chain including clients, professional advisers, contractors, subcontractors and suppliers of materials must be integrated to manage risk and apply value management and engineering techniques to improve buildability and drive waste out of the process'. The report identified that 'Private sector clients are increasingly establishing long-term collaborative relationships or partnering with construction firms for the benefits of both parties – client and supplier'. The benefits include better building design, minimisation of costly design changes, more efficient processes, replication of good practices learned in earlier projects, and a reduction in costly disputes. The report went on to argue that partnering offers good potential to improve the performance of projects in the public sector provided that departments do not have a cosy relationship with contractors which could lead to the risk of less value for money and possible fraud

* The *Achieving Excellence* suite of briefings will replace the *Procurement Guidance* series during 2003. The new series reflects developments in construction procurement over recent years and builds on departments' experience of implementing the Achieving Excellence in Construction initiative.

and impropriety. On the other hand, if partnering is established properly, with robust measures of performance and targets for improvement, commitment to continuous improvement and open-book accounting, it can provide greater assurance that value for money is being achieved.

The report *Accelerating Change*, published in 2002 by the Strategic Forum for Construction, builds on and reaffirms the principles set out in *Rethinking Construction*. Amongst its recommendations the report calls for clients to require the use of 'integrated teams and long term supply chains and actively participate in their creation'. The Forum also recommends that 'Clients, who wish it, have access to independent, expert advice on all the options for meeting their business and project needs. Such advice should cover a range of procurement and management options'.

1.3. Scope of the report and its target audience

This report aims to provide advice for RSLs on the implementation of partnering in its new scheme developments. It is based on the outcomes of the BPiPG's research project, the overall aims of which were to contribute to:

○ defining and understanding partnering and its application to RSL new development activity;
○ establishing the benefits to be derived and the difficulties involved;
○ the development of good practice guidance for practitioners on its adoption and implementation in scheme developments.

The specific objectives of the project were as follows:

○ To identify a framework or model for partnering aimed at adding value for the main stakeholders and removing identified waste.
○ To identify how the determinants of value in development projects for RSLs can be translated, communicated, and used to add value and drive out waste in new-build social housing schemes.
○ To identify the key business relationships and processes operating within the development process that influence the key RSL needs such as quality and whole-life costs.
○ To identify enablers and inhibitors of the application of partnering such as probity, compliance, culture, contractual issues, and technology, both within and between organisations involved in the development of social housing schemes.
○ To identify within specific areas of the development process the most appropriate performance measures, including housing quality indicators (HQIs) and key performance indicators (KPIs), that can be shared between partners as a form of benchmarking to support continuous improvement.
○ To develop ways of collecting data on these appropriate measures to identify where value and waste (i.e. activity that adds no value to the client or end user) is created at each point in the development process.

It needs to be recognised that this report covers only the first stages in developing a partnering approach. The remaining stages of the innovation process of implementing, sustaining and evaluating partnering will be the focus of subsequent reports. It should also be read in conjunction with other key sources of information and advice including the Housing Corporation's *Scheme Development Standards*, published in August 2000 and March 2003, the Housing Corporation's Regulatory

Code, the *Government Construction Procurement Guidance*, produced by HM Treasury and published by the Office for Government Commerce, and *Partnering in the Social Housing Sector*, produced by the European Construction Institute, and published by Thomas Telford Publishing. Details of other publications and guidance may be found in the bibliography section of this report.

1.4. How this report was prepared

This report was prepared as part of a research project co-funded by the Housing Corporation and the members of the BPiPG. The advice it contains was developed from a study of the initial stages of three pilot projects, and an investigation of the

---

The BPiPG's three pilot projects

Sandburrows Walk Knightstone Housing Association
Bristol Churches Housing Association
Turner and Townsend (cost consultant)
Quattro Design (architect)
Bovis Homes (main contractor)

The project is located in Highridge in Bristol. It comprises 25 units. The project commenced in March 2001 and was completed in April 2002. It was undertaken by Knightstone Housing Association (who contracted with Bovis Homes for 12 houses) and Bristol Churches Housing Association (who contracted with Bovis Homes for 13 houses). The employer's requirements, contract terms and conditions were identical, apart from some small differences. The contract value was £825,000 for the Bristol Churches element of the project and £623,000 for the Knightstone element of project.

Clarence Hotel Devon and Cornwall Housing Association
Randall and Simmonds (cost consultant and partnering facilitator)
Midas Homes (designer, main contractor/developer)

The project is located in Torquay. It comprises 28 flats – 14 × 1 bedroom and 14 × 2 bedroom flats. Included within the 28 flats were two flats that had been adapted for wheelchair users. The project was undertaken between September 2000 and January 2002. The project was new build, involving the use of a JCT '98 contract. The project involved the demolition of an existing hotel and the development of the 28 flats on four floors. There was very little room on the site for site facilities and access.

Fortfield Road Guinness Trust Housing Association
Symonds Group (cost consultant)
Leadbitter Construction (main contractor)

The project, which is located in Bristol, was tendered on the basis of four sites all within 100 m of each other but not actually abutting. The project comprises 71 units in total with a total value of £4,312,598. The sites are in a sub-urban area, with the majority of existing properties comprising 1960–1970s semidetached houses. The sites are level and mostly make use of the existing road frontages for access. The schemes consist mainly of new build semi-detached properties, with their own parking within fenced front gardens.

Two prices were obtained at tender stage on the basis of the four sites being carried out either consecutively or sequentially. Due to the allocations received, all four sites were to be constructed consecutively with a start on site in April 2001, thereby making a saving on preliminaries.

---

findings of other research into the development of more collaborative customer–supplier relationships in other sectors of construction, and in other industries.

The research project was managed by Vic O'Brien, of Knightstone Housing Association.* The research methodology was based on action research, which is an essentially practical research method used to solve real-world problems and introduce change aimed at improving current practices.

Action research

In action research the processes of research and action are integrated. It rejects the traditional view of research as a two-stage process in which research is initially carried out by researchers, and then in a separate second stage the knowledge generated by the researchers is applied by practitioners.

In organisational terms, the action research project comprised three groups: the organisations (in the form of senior managers), the subject (the project teams where the change is to take place) and the researcher. These formed the BPiPG, in and through which the research was carried out and the issue of partnering addressed.

The project focused on the roles played by RSLs, consultants and main contractors in adopting partnering. The Construction Industry Training Board advised the team on issues in relation to providing people with the skills and knowledge needed for a successful adoption and implementation of partnering. The members of the research team were responsible for representing other major stakeholders including local authorities, specialist and trade subcontractors, and suppliers. They were also responsible for disseminating the findings from the research project within their own organisations and pilot projects, and to the other stakeholders.

This report is aimed at the main stakeholders in scheme developments in the social housing sector. These include:

O   the Housing Corporation;
O   local authorities;
O   RSLs;
O   design and cost consultants;
O   main contractors and developers;
O   specialist and trade subcontractors;
O   component and materials suppliers.

* Vic O'Brien is now the Director of Western Housing Consultancy Services.

Section 2

Definitions, issues, benefits and concerns

2.1. The performance of construction

A succession of reports into the state of construction has identified its strengths and weaknesses. Its strengths include its flexibility and agility and its workforce that is willing, adaptable and able to work in the harshest conditions. However, a number of reports on construction have identified that, as a whole, construction is underachieving, with considerable scope to improve its productivity, add value for money, and increase client satisfaction and supplier profitability. There is a growing consensus that construction's weaknesses can be attributed to issues on both the demand and supply sides of the industry.

Weaknesses on the demand side in the context of social housing schemes include:

○ the often low and discontinuous demand for development work from RSLs;
○ RSLs' one-off or scheme-by-scheme approach to development;
○ the appointment of consultants and main contractors mainly on the basis of price rather than value;
○ RSLs' contractual and price competitive approach to procurement;
○ RSLs' overly prescriptive and detailed scheme designs and specifications;
○ RSLs' aversion to risk leading to its often inappropriate allocation and management;
○ the sector's protracted and complex planning, feasibility and funding processes;
○ the limited availability of suitable sites for development, and their price;
○ the uncertainties and inefficiencies resulting from the Housing Corporation's annual funding cycle and the periodic changes in policy direction and levels of investment.

On the supply side of social housing schemes these weaknesses include:

○ the main contractor's appointment of specialist and trade subcontractors on the basis of price rather than value;
○ fragmented and transient supply chains which are poorly integrated with project processes;
○ the lack of understanding of the values, needs and aspirations of RSLs and their tenants;
○ the number of defects and disappointing quality;
○ the lack of price and time certainty;
○ low barriers to main and subcontractor entry;
○ severe price competition but limited quality competition;
○ low profit margins;
○ poor public image leading to recruitment problems;
○ the late and limited involvement of specialist and trade subcontractors and suppliers.

There are also a number of common issues which need to be addressed, including:

○ the sector's contractual relationships and adversarial culture;
○ the fragmented development process and poorly integrated supply chains;
○ the lack of coordination and integration of the overall process;
○ inadequate investment in research and development, learning and innovation;
○ the overall lack of focus on the needs of external and internal customers.

2.2. The drivers for change in construction

Sir Michael Latham's report, *Constructing the Team*, published in 1994, and Sir John Egan's report, *Rethinking Construction*, published in 1998, set out a challenging agenda for change in construction – including the housebuilding sector. The Egan report, whilst acknowledging that some parts of construction were world class, concluded that most of the industry was underperforming, particularly in terms of cost, quality and time, and that it should:

○ more closely meet the needs and expectations of end users;
○ move away from traditional contractual and confrontational ways of doing business to more collaborative approaches;
○ aim to achieve performance improvement targets for reduction in costs, time, accidents and defects, and increases in predictability of cost and time, productivity and profitability.

The report also recognised the specificity of housing by concluding that it is affected by some significant factors that distinguish it from other sectors of the construction industry, including the planning process, the availability and price of land, and the uncertainties and inefficiencies resulting from periodic changes in policy direction and levels of investment. Nevertheless, from 2000 to 2001, in common with all government expenditure on construction, social housing grants have been linked to Egan compliance. The Housing Corporation responded in 2000 by redrafting its SDSs to 'introduce the cultural and procedural changes necessary to better enable RSLs wishing to embrace the principles contained in the report of the Government's Construction Task Force'. The Egan compliance measures, introduced by the Housing Corporation in the 2001–2002 funding round, included the use of KPIs, HQIs and a commitment to partnering.

2.3. What is partnering?

Partnering, which began to emerge in the UK in the late 1980s, can be seen as construction's attempt to emulate business practice in other sectors of the economy and break down the barriers between the main project participants by developing closer, more collaborative relationships between them. It was given considerable impetus by the publication of the Latham Report in 1994 and by Sir John Egan's Construction Task Force, with the publication of its report, *Rethinking Construction*, in 1998, which identified 'partnering in the supply chain' as one of its four priorities for change. From the late 1990s onwards, central government, through HM Treasury and more recently the Office of Government Commerce, has issued a number of guidance notes advocating the use of partnering as a way of yielding 'significant savings in time and cost'. More recently, the concept was given further momentum by the publication of the report *Accelerating Change*, which was published in 2002 by the Strategic Forum for Construction, which recommended that clients 'use integrated teams and long term supply chains and actively participate in their creation'.

> In the report *Rethinking Construction*, partnering is defined as: 'two or more organisations working together to improve performance through agreeing mutual objectives, devising a way of resolving any disputes and committing themselves to continuous improvement, measuring progress and sharing the gains'.

Partnering is a much-used term with a number of definitions and interpretations. This is because it takes many different forms, which have been developed through an evolutionary rather than a systematic process. To some, it is often used to describe good project management or teamwork. For others, it means a long-term strategic alliance. This shows that partnering is not a unified concept. It takes a number of different forms, including: project partnering; post-award project partnering; semi-project partnering; pre-selection arrangement; coordination arrangement; and strategic or full partnering. This explains the number of definitions of partnering and the confusion in relation to what it really means and entails. The primary definition of partnering appears to have been developed by the Construction Industry Institute's Partnering Task Force, which defines partnering as:

> a long-term commitment between two or more organisations for the purpose of achieving specific business objectives by maximising the effectiveness of each participant's resources. The relationship is based on trust, dedication to common goals, and an understanding of each other's individual expectations and values.

The Reading Construction Forum has defined it as follows:

> Partnering is a managerial approach used by two or more organisations to achieve specific business objectives by maximising the effectiveness of each participant's resources. The approach is based on mutual objectives, an agreed method of problem resolution and an active search for continuous measurable improvements.

Although there are similarities between these two definitions there are also significant differences. A more recent definition was provided by the Construction

Industry Board (Working Group 12), which builds on the Latham Report and the work of the Reading Construction Forum. It states that:

> Partnering is a structured management approach to facilitate teamworking across contractual boundaries. It should not be confused with other good project management practice, or with long-standing relationships, negotiated contracts, or preferred supplier arrangements, all of which lack the structure and objective measures that must support a partnering relationship.

Again there are similarities and differences. In the last definition, as well as references to what partnering is, there are also indications of what it is not. This could be seen as indicating that some approaches labelled as partnering should not be classified as partnering. An analysis of these and other definitions and the considerable literature on partnering shows that it is a much-used term with many definitions and interpretations. It also shows that construction's perception of partnering has evolved since its introduction in the late 1980s. This means that as there is no single definition or model that is appropriate to all situations, all partnering approaches are to some extent different in terms of, for example, scope, aims, objectives, duration, value systems, content, focus, adoption, implementation and outcomes. This has resulted in the term often being misused and the concept misunderstood.

One significant area where misunderstanding exists is differentiating partnering from teamworking. *Government Construction Procurement Guidance*, provided by the Office of Government Commerce, attempts to clarify the difference between teamworking and partnering. Teamwork involves:

○ openness about expectations and returns;
○ alignment of objectives;
○ mutual benefit from the agreed outcome.

On the other hand, partnering involves more *formal* structures to be agreed by the parties which:

○ identify the common goals for success;
○ set out a common resolution ladder for reaching decisions and solving problems;
○ identify the targets that provide measurable continuous improvement;
○ provide 'gain and pain' share arrangements (rewards and incentives and not just money).

These should be set out in a partnering charter and arrangements, which should not replace the need for a formal contract. The approach to partnering should also fit the circumstances of the specific situation. This indicates that partnering should be seen as going beyond the normal project management and teamwork associated with construction projects by the inclusion of more organised and formal efforts to:

○ reduce conflict and the need to resort to litigation;
○ improve communication;
○ increase quality and add value;
○ increase profitability;
○ build greater trust between the parties.

The existence of the many different definitions and types of partnering can be explained mainly by the diversity of construction's clients, and the varying levels of collaboration and integration that are possible in different situations. However, there is now a growing consensus on the core characteristics of partnering, including:

○ the need for commitment from senior management;
○ mutual objectives;
○ an agreed method for resolving problems;
○ continuous measurable improvement.

Some other characteristics, such as long-term relationships and mutual competitive advantage, are, however, much more contentious and difficult to realise in the context of construction.

Also, there is growing consensus on the way in which the many forms of partnering can be classified – mainly in terms of their scope and stages of evolution. Work by the Reading Construction Forum suggests three generations of partnering: 'first generation', 'second generation' and, more recently, 'third generation' partnering. As shown in Figure 2.1, first-generation partnering began to emerge in the late 1980s in a number of sectors of the industry, but mainly in the retail and offshore oil and gas industries.

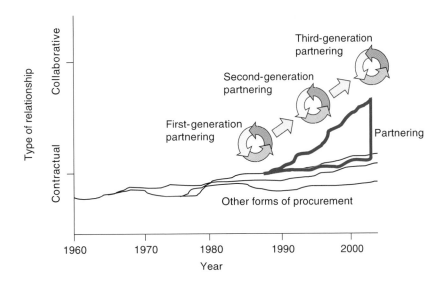

Fig. 2.1. The evolution of partnering

These early ideas on partnering revolved around three key principles, which were applied within individual projects on a project-by-project basis:

○ agreeing mutual objectives to take into account the interests of all the firms involved;
○ making decisions openly and resolving problems in a way that was jointly agreed at the start of the project;
○ aiming at targets that provide measurable improvements in performance from previous projects.

This form of partnering recognises the difficulties of building long-term relationships between clients and main contractors in much of project-based construction. It is also often argued as being particularly well suited to public sector procurement, given the risk-averse culture of its project owners and sponsors, and many constraints such as the need to demonstrate probity, value for money and public accountability. Although this basic form of partnering has been shown to provide some benefits, it has limited scope for developing the close relationships and integrated processes, which are necessary for the substantial performance improvements seen in some other industries. However, encouraged by the early success of first-generation partnering, leading-edge private-sector clients and their construction partners have progressed to second-generation partnering and extended their relationships with consultants, main contractors and other key suppliers beyond the duration of a specific project to a period of time or a number of projects. This provided the opportunity to address the limitations of project-specific partnering by building relationships and integrating and improving processes over a longer period. This progression from project-specific to strategic partnering is as shown in Figure 2.2.

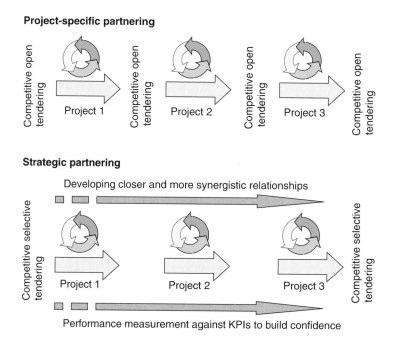

Fig. 2.2. *The progression from project-specific to strategic partnering*

This progression to strategic partnering provided the opportunity to address the limitations of project-specific partnering by building more synergistic and collaborative relationships and improving processes over a longer period of time than that associated with project-by-project tendering. This allowed the three key objectives of first-generation partnering to be extended to include:

○ *Joint strategy development*: identifying and satisfying the objectives of the client and end users and their key suppliers.
○ *Appropriate membership*: selecting and involving the most appropriate organisations and business units to ensure all necessary skills and knowledge are available and developed.
○ *Equity*: ensuring everyone is rewarded for their work on the basis of fair prices and profits.

○ *Integration*: improving the way in which the organisations and business units involved work together by rationalising roles and processes and having the appropriate interface structures in place.

○ *Joint performance measurement*: setting measurable targets to support continuous improvement and benchmark progress against other partnerships in the same and different settings.

Establishment of closer, longer-term and more synergistic relationships associated with this more advanced form of partnering is part of the Rethinking Construction movement. The main objective is to increase the certainty that the client's needs are met, and that all those who have contributed to the process feel adequately rewarded for their efforts. It recognises the mutual interdependence that exists between construction organisations and the need to reduce the blame culture that pervades much of the industry. In its most advanced forms it offers a means to avoid unnecessary and costly repeated selection of new teams, which inhibit collective learning, innovation, investment and the development of skills and experience. The longer-term customer–supplier relationships, with suppliers being chosen according to the value they can add for the end user as well as price, allows the development of teams that work together synergistically to improve performance through a number of projects.

What do construction practitioners think about partnering?

Masons' solicitors recently undertook a survey on partnering in the UK construction industry, *Partnering – the Industry Speaks*. The report is based on a survey carried out at the firm's Annual Construction Law Conferences. Over 1000 delegates from 150 companies at seven centres across the UK were asked to give their views on the impact of partnering on their business as well as their assessment of the risks and key benefits of this new method of procurement.

The breakdown of respondents was as follows:

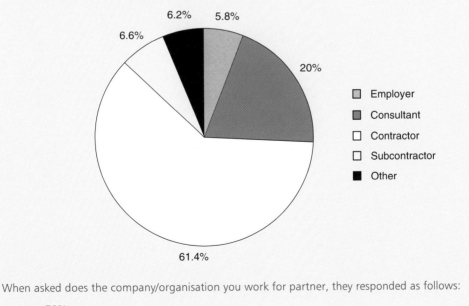

When asked does the company/organisation you work for partner, they responded as follows:

○ yes, 79%;
○ no, 17.7%;
○ unsure, 3.3%.

What do construction practitioners think about partnering? (Contd)

The respondents identified the following pitfalls of partnering:

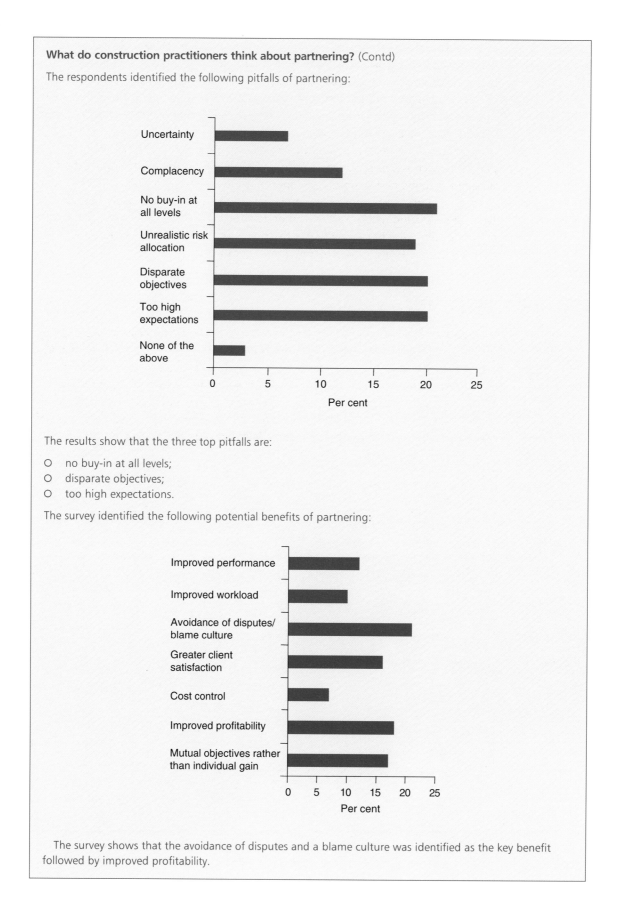

The results show that the three top pitfalls are:

O   no buy-in at all levels;
O   disparate objectives;
O   too high expectations.

The survey identified the following potential benefits of partnering:

The survey shows that the avoidance of disputes and a blame culture was identified as the key benefit followed by improved profitability.

More recently there has been considerable progress in establishing a more consistent and systematic approach to introducing partnering into a number of construction sectors, including social housing. This has been supported by strong leadership andcommitment from the Housing Corporation and with the publication of guidance such as the handbook *Partnering in the Social Housing Sector*, and the launch of PPC 2000, the first standard partnering contract.

In conclusion, it can be seen that there is no single definition or model of partnering that is appropriate to all situations. All approaches are to some extent different in terms of, for example, scope, aims, objectives, participants, value systems, content, focus, adoption, implementation and outcomes. However, all types of partnering have a common characteristic in that they endeavour to promote a more positive and synergistic relationship between the parties, but most particularly between the client and the main contractor.

2.4. The benefits of partnering

Through partnering, construction's regular and frequent private-sector clients and their consultants and contractors have begun to demonstrate the benefits of establishing a more open and collaborative business environment based upon mutual objectives, joint decision-making and continuous improvement, rather than the opportunistic behaviour, hierarchical decision-making and lack of ongoing improvement traditionally associated with construction. Using first-generation partnering, these early adopters of the concept in the private sector, such as Whitbread and Pearce Retail, have

---

The experience of Whitbread

Through partnering with Pearce Leisure, Whitbread has achieved substantial measurable improvements in performance in its hotel development programme.

Improved value for money for Whitbread:

1996   Output 2 bedrooms per week
           Overall cost of development £43,000 per room
1997   Output 3 bedrooms per week
           Overall cost of development £29,000 per room
1999   Output 5 bedrooms per week
           Overall cost of development £23,000 per room

Improved business results for Pearce Leisure:

Turnover up 100%
Net profit nearly doubled
Overheads up only 50%
Productivity per employee up from £790,000 to £836,000

This was achieved through:

O   careful selection of partners – not just price based;
O   using fewer suppliers in long-term relationships;
O   developing greater customer focus through more specialisation and improved communication with end users;
O   simplifying products and processes;
O   increasing openness, transparency and trust;
O   measuring and driving progress through performance measures.

---

demonstrated that although it is difficult to implement and sustain, it can provide substantial improvements for clients and suppliers.

The benefits from these more collaborative approaches include:

○ better communication and more sharing of information, which can lead to more open decision-making and the better identification and management of risk;

○ more transparent procedures and processes leading to greater clarity in terms of 'who' does 'what', 'where', 'when', 'how' and, increasingly, 'why' in projects and their supply chains;

○ the gradual development of better ways of working leading to more integrated processes and systems;

○ greater transparency in business transactions, decision-making and the allocation of risk leading to greater trust and commitment;

○ increased focus on the needs of both internal and external customers;

○ more effective teamworking leading to increased synergy and buildability, better risk management, and increased certainty of out-turn results in relation to quality, cost and time and other key performance indicators;

○ cost reductions and/or added value across the whole-life cycle of the project;

○ optimal selection and specification of equipment, components and materials;

○ increased collective learning arising from joint problem-solving leading to better decision-making, more understanding of the whole process, increased trust and greater commitment;

○ more innovation in products and processes related to delivering greater end user value and enhanced whole-life performance;

○ greater inter-supply chain competitiveness and responsiveness to changes in the external environment;

○ more continuity of work and more predictable profit margins for main contractors and their suppliers.

Although examples from a number of sectors of construction demonstrate the considerable benefits to be derived from the effective implementation of partnering – especially in the more advanced forms where it has been possible for the main parties to develop closer, more open, stable and longer-term collaborative relationships – it must be recognised that there are also major strategic consequences, difficulties, and real and perceived barriers to be addressed. These can include:

○ differences in the aims, objectives, processes and cultures of the organisations involved;

○ multiple and often hidden goals and continuing opportunistic behaviour;

○ power imbalances and abuses in the new relationship;

○ differences in values and language;

○ incompatible collaborative capabilities;

○ the tension between allowing greater autonomy for suppliers and yet retaining some form of control and accountability;

○ the considerable investment in time and resources needed to build closer and more open relationships, to change organisational cultures, and develop the assets of the partnership;

○ the risks associated with overdependency on fewer suppliers and customers;

○ restricted access to new technologies and management approaches.

Some warnings

An investigation of UK partnering practices across a number of sectors of the economy warns that companies that ignore the realities of their commercial situation and assume that a partnering approach is universally applicable face ultimate disappointment. The report found a number of factors which militate against successful partnering, including:

O   conflicting buyer and supplier objectives in critical areas of the relationship;
O   a lack of commitment to building mutual competitive advantage;
O   inconsistent and continuing opportunistic behaviour throughout the partnering organisations.

There are also concerns associated with partnering in the context and culture of the social housing sector. Most notably its complex and protracted planning processes, the availability and price of land, and the uncertainties and inefficiencies resulting from periodic changes in policy direction and levels of investment. These can be seen as major barriers to RSLs as they seek to generate the volume and continuity of work needed to develop and sustain the long-term, open and more collaborative customer–supplier relationships associated with the more advanced forms of partnering.

Section 3

The BPiPG's model for partnering

The BPiPG has developed a mode l of partnering in the context of the social housing sector. This is based on good practice evidence from the research findings and from the experiences of partnering in other construction sectors and other industries. The model sets out the main elements of a sustainable partnering approach for RSLs in their scheme developments. It also proposes a number of actions needed to implement the main elements of the model and the main barriers to be overcome if it is to be successful.

The model reflects the growing understanding that partnering is a multifactor innovation that needs to be implemented in a way that fits the specificity of RSLs, the needs of their tenants, their scheme developments and associated supply chains. The extent to which it can be implemented in an RSL's supply chain depends on the level of influence that that a particular RSL has over its suppliers and the degree of collaboration and mutual advantage that is possible. There are considerable challenges in bringing about the cultural changes needed to begin developing closer, more open and collaborative interorganisational relationships and drive out opportunistic behaviour. This means it needs to be implemented over a considerable period of time and in a number of phases.

Evidence from other sectors also indicates that the organisations embarking on partnering need to ensure that their internal organisational structures and culture are conducive to partnering before embarking on the development of closer interorganisational relationships. Partnering should not, therefore, be seen as an easy and instant panacea for all the social housing sector's problems. There are a number of prerequisites, difficulties, disappointments, setbacks and indeed new conflicts to be addressed in adopting, implementing and sustaining such a radical new approach. It demands an openness and honesty that is not always evident in the traditional relationships between the main parties in construction. Finally, it also acknowledges that although the partners will not have the same objectives it will only work if each partner derives its fair share of the benefits from its adoption and implementation.

3.1. The roots of more collaborative approaches

Traditionally, most organisations have viewed themselves as entities that exist independently from others, and indeed need to compete with each other in order to survive. However, since the mid-1980s, more and more organisations have sought to change their external relationships by developing closer and more harmonious links with their suppliers and customers. This has been in response to the new competitive paradigm, or model, that increasingly places the organisation at the centre of interdependent supply chains – a confederation of mutually complementary competencies and capabilities – which competes as an integrated supply chain against other supply chains rather than as individual entities.

> **What is a paradigm?**
>
> As far as its applicability to organisations is concerned, a paradigm can be defined as a way of looking at and interpreting the world: a framework of basic assumptions, theories and models that are commonly and strongly accepted and shared within a particular field of activity at a particular point in time.
>
> It is important to recognise, however, that as situations change and people's perceptions change, existing paradigms lose their relevance and new ones emerge.

It is becoming clear that to manage in such a radically revised competitive structure requires different skills and priorities to those employed in the traditional price-competitive model. To achieve success in the world of supply chain competition necessitates a focus on supply chain management as well as upon the management of internal processes.

> **Supply chains**
>
> Supply chains comprise all those business units that have to interact in order to get a product or service to the end user or customer.

> **Supply chain management (SCM)**
>
> This is the management of upstream and downstream relationships with suppliers and customers to deliver superior customer value at less cost to the supply chain as a whole. Thus, it focuses on the management of relationships in order to achieve a more profitable outcome for *all* parties in the chain.

The evidence from those industries that have had more experience of supply chain competition and management suggests a number of key factors in the development of closer and more collaborative relationships:

○ The move to more stable and collaborative relationships between customers and suppliers is not merely a case of adjustments at the interfaces between the organisations involved. To be successful, it also requires more fundamental changes deep within both the customer and supplier organisations, including attitudinal and structural changes.

○ Although closer relationships between organisations in the supply chain can bring benefits these can be limited, and indeed jeopardised, if they are not accompanied by closer strategic relationships and joint strategy development.

○ Some firms have enhanced these supply chain relationships by assisting their suppliers to improve their performance. This has involved them in going beyond exhortation to become directly involved in the process of change within supplier organisations.

○ There are examples to show that the move to develop new relationships need not just be driven by customers, as some suppliers have successfully persuaded their customers to enter into a partnership and more collaborative relationships.

○ A major benefit of closer interorganisational relationships within supply chains is that they can play a significant role in helping the organisations to cope with turbulence, uncertainty, changing customer needs and shifts in their market and wider environments.

○ It is difficult for organisations to quantify in advance the benefits of developing closer and more collaborative interorganisational relationships and partnerships. This implies that the move to new customer–supplier relationships is not always driven by rational and quantitative decision-making and often requires a step of faith by the organisations involved.

Of the many issues and challenges facing organisations as they make the transition to this new competitive environment, the evidence from other industries suggests the following are perhaps the most significant:

○ Collective strategy development – traditionally members of supply chains have not shared with each other their strategic thinking. For supply chain competition to be truly effective, the members must collectively agree strategic goals for the whole supply chain and the means of attaining them.

○ Win–win thinking – one of the biggest challenges is to break away from the often adversarial nature of buyer–supplier relationships that have characterised interorganisational relationships in the past. If partnering is to be successful, all partners need to benefit from, and be better off as a result of, the greater collaboration.

○ Open communication – one of the most powerful drivers of change in supply chains in other industries has been better and more open communication between supply chain partners. Open-book accounting is a manifestation of this move towards transparency by which cost data are shared upstream and downstream in the supply chain and hence each partner's profit is visible to the others. Knowledge management and the advent of information technology have provided further means of acquiring and sharing data, information and knowledge between supply chain partners.

Given the timing of the adoption of partnering by the BPiPG, it has also benefited from the experiences of other construction sectors as they have attempted to emulate other industries and move towards closer, more harmonious customer–

supplier relationships. In particular, the model has been strongly influenced by the experienced gained by the early pioneers of partnering in the retail and offshore sectors of the industry. Several features of its approach have also been built on some of the positive characteristics of the 'design and build', 'design and construct' and 'construction management' procurement methods. The BPiPG's model will also be familiar to those organisations that are using 'business excellence' as a means to improve performance. Its emphasis on the whole-life cycle and maximising functionality also bears some resemblance to private finance initiative projects and prime contracting. The importance attached to adding value and the reduction of waste also resonates with the principles of lean construction. Hence, the BPiPG considers that its more holistic approach to partnering incorporates features that reflect the growing understanding of the complexity of developing more collaborative longer-ter customer–supplier relationships. It also acknowledges the significant number of factors involved in successful partnering, as well as recognising the need for a more systematic approach to its implementation that closely reflects the specificity of the client's needs and their supply systems.

3.2. Adding value and increasing mutual competitive advantage

In the new competitive paradigm outlined above, supply chain competes with supply chain and the success of each organisation will depend upon how well the supply chain is managed as a whole. Continuous improvement activities aimed at driving out waste, adding value and sharing rewards should result in mutual competitive advantage. This creation of greater value through mutual competitive advantage is at the heart of the BPiPG's approach. For this to work the members of the supply chain need to identify their external and internal customers and to be absolutely clear as to what they truly value.

Setting the right targets

Before embarking on partnering the members of the BPiPG used the HQIs and the 10 headline KPIs to identify what constituted value for RSLs and their tenants.

They undertook retrospective analyses of three previously completed schemes using HQIs and the 10 headline KPIs to measure the effectiveness of traditional approaches in delivering value. These scores set down markers against which performance improvements to add value as a result of partnering could be measured.

Taking the example of cost certainty or predictability, which is very important to housing associations, Knightstone selected a previous scheme that was built within £3000 of its target cost of £2 million. A metric for cost certainty was set up to measure variance around a target cost. A target was set at 10% below the benchmarked total (i.e. in line with Housing Corporation targets) but adjusted by the employer's agent to allow for differences in the schemes such as ground conditions. The metric was set up so that any 10% reduction or increase from the adjusted benchmark figure is treated as a negative variance. This is illustrated below:

0%	50%	100%
£1.8 million	£1.89 million	£1.98 million
	£1.71 million	£1.62 million

Setting the right targets (contd)

This metric was then combined with the other headline KPIs in a radar diagram:

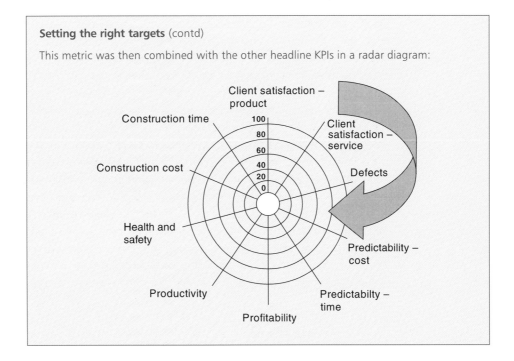

Having established what constitutes value for the end user and each organisation in the supply chain, the partners need to develop a clear understanding of the supply chain in order to establish which activities add value, which activities are non-value-adding and those activities that are non-value-adding but necessary.

The different forms of activities

Value-adding activities are those activities that add value in the eyes of the end user and make a product or service more valuable.

Non-value-adding activities are those that, in the eyes of the end user, do not make a product or service more valuable and are not necessary even under present circumstances. These activities are 'waste' and should be targeted for early removal.

Necessary non-value-adding activities are those that do not make a product or service more valuable but are necessary unless the existing supply process is radically changed. Such waste is more difficult to remove in the short term and should be a target for longer-term or more radical change.

Wastes include defects, waiting, unnecessary inventory, inappropriate processing, excessive transport and unnecessary motion.

In the context of social housing projects, the end users of scheme developments include the tenants and the RSL's housing management and technical services departments. However, it also needs to be recognised that there are internal customers within the scheme development process and supply chains, and that they will have needs and things that they value. These internal customers include the individuals and business units who receive the work of others and add their contribution to the product or service before passing it to someone else in the development process. In the case of social housing, these will include the Housing Corporation, consultants, contractors, specialist and trade subcontractors, and suppliers. If there is no clear perception of who these customers are in the first place, then it is unlikely that there will be a clear perception of their needs either. If, on the other hand, the internal customers' requirements are agreed and met, a chain of improvements is made that reach out to the end users – the tenants – as shown in Figure 3.1.

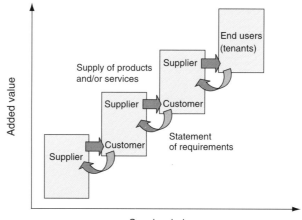

Fig. 3.1. *The customer–supplier value chain*

This customer-oriented approach is designed to deliver the greatest possible value to all the key stakeholders and provide benefits for all the parties involved. The advantage accruing to the RSL and its tenants should be greater value for money in the areas that matter most to them, such as:

○ sustainable developments;
○ higher HQI scores at the same or lower cost;
○ lower maintenance and whole-life costs;
○ reduction of running costs for tenants;
○ lower carbon dioxide emissions;
○ appropriate use of local labour;
○ greater tenant satisfaction.

For the consultants, contractors and their suppliers, value means:

○ maintaining or growing their market share;
○ continuity of work;
○ enhancing reputation for quality of products and/or services;
○ delivering more predictable and higher profit margins.

For the team as a whole it means the opportunity to:

○ integrate value and risk management across the whole development process;
○ raise the quality of the end product and its buildability;
○ improve working conditions and interpersonal relationships within the supply chain;
○ reduce conflicts;
○ increase synergy;
○ maintain or lower costs through the removal of waste; and, therefore,
○ provide a framework for achieving better value for money.

Sustainable development

Sustainable development was defined by the Brundtland Report in 1987 as 'Development that meets the needs of the present without compromising the ability of future generations to meet their own needs'. The key facets of sustainable development are:

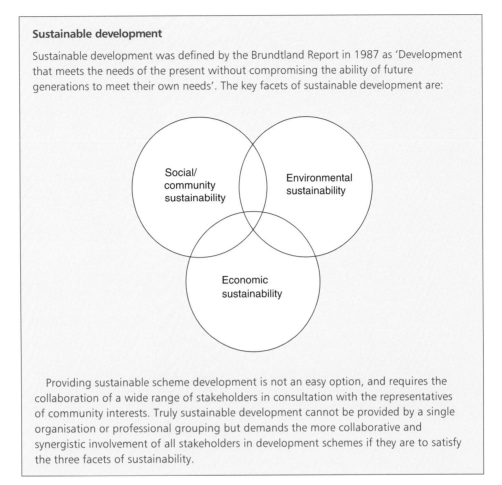

Providing sustainable scheme development is not an easy option, and requires the collaboration of a wide range of stakeholders in consultation with the representatives of community interests. Truly sustainable development cannot be provided by a single organisation or professional grouping but demands the more collaborative and synergistic involvement of all stakeholders in development schemes if they are to satisfy the three facets of sustainability.

Value for money

According to the Office of Government Commerce, value for money is the optimum combination of whole-life cost and quality to meet customer's requirements. This requires:

O   defining the project carefully to meet user needs;
O   integrating value and risk management techniques within normal project management;
O   adopting a change control procedure;
O   taking account of whole-life costing;
O   avoiding waste and conflict through teamworking and partnering;
O   appointing consultants and contractors on the basis of value for money rather than lowest initial price;
O   a framework for achieving value for money.

3.3. Continuous improvement

Constantly delivering greater value and increasing mutual competitive advantage implies continuous improvement, the concept and practice of which are well established in other industries. The aim is to create a culture that results in an endless process of improvement. It is now widely accepted that the 'quality miracle' by Japanese manufacturing industry in the post-war years owes much to what they term *kaizen*, or continuous improvement.

Continuous improvement

Kaizen is the bottom-up capability developed by Toyota, Canon and others that involves the entire workforce in improvement-oriented planning, execution and control. The central idea reflects the Japanese penchant for concentrating on people and processes rather than products and organisation.

The main weakness of *kaizen* is that it can be too inward-looking and not responsive enough to strong forces of change. 'Intrapreneurship' provides an alternative approach, which involves bottom–up entrepreneurial activity in a direct response to market opportunities. Some American companies, including 3M and Hewlett Packard, have used this approach to considerable effect.

Kaizen, it can be argued, is more appropriate than 'intrapreneurship' in continuously improving in the context and risk-averse culture of social housing.

Although relatively unfamiliar to the construction industry, continuous improvement is well established in other industries. It is a way of achieving long-term performance improvement, in terms of what is delivered to the end user and the profitability to suppliers. The two main elements of continuous improvement are doing things 'right first time' and utilising the contributions of everyone involved. In practice this means paying greater attention to planning how to do things in advance and determining how problems can be anticipated and avoided. It also means recognising the significance of the knowledge and expertise of practitioners at the operational level because they have a detailed understanding of how the work is done and how it could be improved. While top management should endorse and initiate the change and set overall objectives and targets for improvement, it is often at the operational level that the expertise to improve the process resides. Teamwork is, therefore, a key element of continuous improvement philosophy, with teams assuming responsibility for the individual operations they perform and for the proper coordination of these operations, and being empowered to make experiments and changes to improve the process. In this approach the roles of supervisors and managers change as they become team coaches making sure that the teams are motivated and have the resources needed to deliver products and services in a way that meets improvement targets.

The main advantages of continuous improvement are that it can release enormous potential, motivate workers and deliver gains, which while small in the short term can be very significant when accumulated over time. A further advantage is that it also presents lower risks than more radical innovations. However, it must be appreciated that to implement changes in this way can take many years. It requires a change of culture, and many managers find it difficult to shift from being hierarchical bosses to their new role as coaches and facilitators. Typical mistakes include training workers for too long before giving them the tools to use, and expecting very high gains in a short period of time. Also, if not managed properly and not linked to business objectives and supply chain objectives, continuous improvement can lead to doing the wrong things very efficiently.

In the past, continuous improvement has been difficult in construction because of its price-competitive tendering, low and discontinuous demand, fragmentation, temporary and unique project processes, and short-term and often adversarial relationships. In recent years, however, regular clients of the industry with significant and ongoing construction programmes have been using their leverage over their suppliers to assemble more stable supply chains and create the kind of ongoing interorganisational relationships and integrated and repetitive processes that are more conducive to continuous improvement.

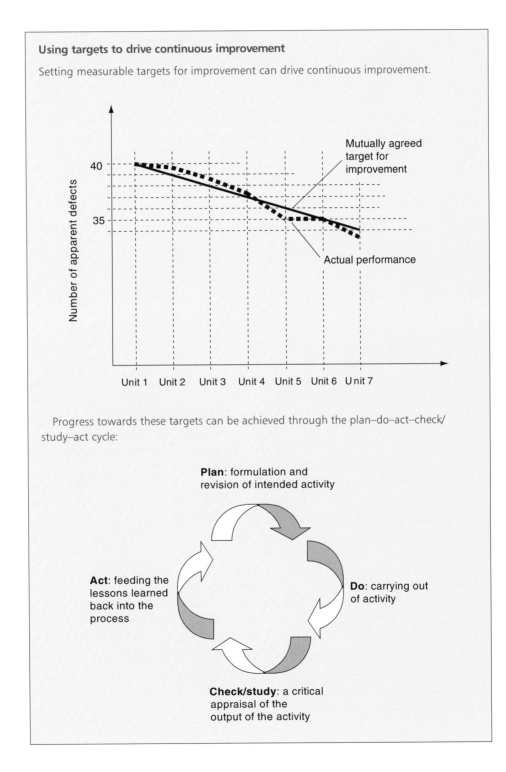

Using targets to drive continuous improvement

Setting measurable targets for improvement can drive continuous improvement.

Progress towards these targets can be achieved through the plan–do–act–check/study–act cycle:

3.4. The elements of the model

The BPiPG's model, shown in Figure 3.2, is designed to drive continuous improvement within a strategic partnering approach aimed at adding value for the end user and building competitive advantage for all the partners. The model comprises seven interrelated elements, which should be seen as the main ingredients of a more systematic approach to the development of more collaborative relationships and integrated processes rather than consecutive steps in a rigid procedure. It must be stressed that the model does not seek to be prescriptive for all RSLs and their development programmes. The ways in which the partners respond to the model should reflect the specificity of the RSL's development programme, its experience of project-specific partnering, and the specific nature of the relationship being developed. Also, in practice, the process of building a partnering approach moves forwards and backwards through these elements in an iterative rather than cyclical way. At any one time you would expect some activity to be going on in each of the elements of the model.

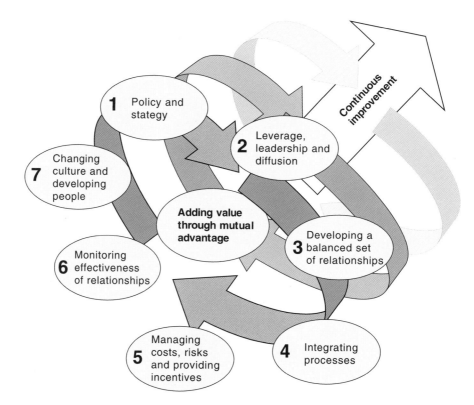

Fig. 3.2. *The seven elements of the BPiPG's model to continuously add value through mutual advantage*

The seven elements can be seen as addressing the main areas for improvement in current practices in new-build scheme developments. As such, the overall approach represents a significant departure from the objectives, relationships, attitudes, behaviours, norms and procedures associated with most current procurement methods, including the more basic forms of project-specific partnering. Adopting the more advanced forms of partnering in this systematic and holistic way is a challenging undertaking, which means breaking with much of what might, in the past, have been seen as important in the business relationships between the key participants in social housing development projects. However, the BPiPG contends that all of these elements need to be addressed to some extent if the more advanced forms of partnering are to be genuine, meaningful and deliver significant performance improvements. If one or more of the elements are omitted, then partnering is unlikely to be successful and sustainable.

Although this may seem a daunting agenda for change for many RSLs and their suppliers, the experience of the BPiPG suggests that the parties need only to make relatively small incremental improvements in each of the seven main elements to start building relationships and demonstrate tangible improvements in performance.

This report does not set out to explain in detail how to set up project-specific partnering arrangements; such advice already exists. For example, the European Construction Institute (ECI) provides helpful advice on the first steps in deciding whether to partner, what form to adopt, and what implementation strategies to adopt in their publication *Partnering in the Social Housing Sector* (published by Thomas Telford Publishing).

Mechanisms of partnering

The ECI publication *Partnering in the Social Housing Sector* provides three 'mechanisms' for adopting partnering:

(1) The partnering decision mechanism, including:

- deciding if and how to partner;
- the role of workshops in the change process;
- gaining commitment from the top;
- the role of the strategy meeting;
- preparing a company charter;
- the role of the partnering champion;
- promoting partnering through the management workshop;
- driving the process forward through a steering group.

(2) The partnering selection mechanism, including:

- the forms of partnering;
- procurement procedure;
- the selection task force;
- the invitation to tender;
- the questionnaire;
- the shortlist;
- interviews;
- debriefing of unsuccessful tenderers.

(3) The partnering implementation mechanism, including:

- the strategy meeting;
- the initial partnering workshop;
- the partnering charter and agreement;
- dispute avoidance;
- monitoring the performance of the partnering process;
- the mediation panel.

Element 1. Policy and strategy – setting the direction and allocating the resources

The first and key decision that has to be made by RSLs and their potential partners is whether partnering is appropriate for them and their scheme developments. In order to make this decision the RSLs and their potential partners will need to:

○ understand partnering in its more advanced forms, the benefits it can bring, and also the challenges associated with its successful implementation;

○ review honestly and objectively the effectiveness of their current approaches to scheme development in satisfying economic, social and environmental requirements;

○ review their external environment and the pressures for change including the current emphasis on more collaborative and integrated procurement approaches to deliver best value schemes;

○ review their own internal receptiveness for more collaborative and integrated working and their preparedness for partnering;

○ assess the degree of influence that individual or clusters of RSLs have in the supply chains to their scheme developments by virtue of the volume, value and continuity of their development programmes.

As a result of this process of learning and review, RSLs and their potential partners should develop growing awareness of partnering and the circumstances in which it will be implemented. This growing knowledge should allow RSLs and their suppliers to decide whether the more advanced forms of partnering are for them, and to select the most appropriate form that best fits their particular circumstances. The adoption and implementation of the selected form of partnering should then be planned. Given the strategic implications of the more advanced forms of partnering, the BPiPG recommends that the partnering approach be introduced on an experimental basis in pilot projects. Over a period of time its effectiveness can be evaluated, and if necessary it can be adapted and modified before being brought into full operation. The innovation cycle is then completed by subsequent reviews and internal audits, which can be used to evaluate the approach and, if necessary, reshape it in response to new factors in the external and internal environment and the growing understanding of factors within and between the organisations involved. This process of implementation is shown in Figure 3.3.

This implementation process shows that there are a number of stages or phases in implementing any innovation – particularly if, as in the case of partnering in its more advanced forms, the innovation is significant. Each of the phases shown in Figure 3.3 is important and must not be rushed. This means that adopting and implementing an innovation on the scale of the most advanced forms of partnering can take considerable time. For example, although the pioneers of partnering, such as some of the leading supermarket chains, have been developing and enhancing their approaches to partnering since the mid-1990s, most would acknowledge that considerable progress still remains to be made.

Developing the policy and strategy for a partnering approach needs to be based both on a review of the external business environment and on an internal audit of the RSL's supply chain's readiness and preparedness for partnering. It involves developing a shared vision of partnering within the RSL's organisation and with the other partners in the relationship. It means coming to specific agreements on its

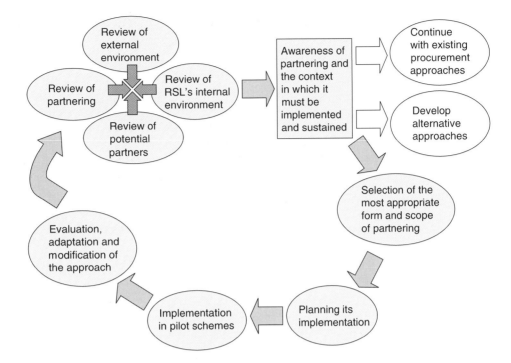

Fig. 3.3. A process for the implementation of partnering

scope and the nature and pace of its implementation. Initially, it requires communicating the approach internally to employees and departments and engaging them in the strategy to implement the partnering plan, and committing the time and resources needed to make it work. Subsequently it needs to be communicated to partner consultants and contractors and other key suppliers of products and services.

Currently, the drivers for change in the external environment include, for example, increasing tenant expectations, the social housing sector's increasing emphasis on quality criteria, the government's focus on best value, and the Housing Corporation's strong commitment to the agenda set out in the Egan Report, *Rethinking Construction*. This external review is also likely to identify the various ways in which supply chain competition, partnering and other more collaborative approaches are developing in other sectors of construction, and indeed other industries. Also, this evaluation of the RSLs external environment will determine the current state of its relationships with its suppliers and the amount of leverage it has over them now, and in the medium to longer term. An assessment of the RSL's internal environment is needed to gauge its readiness for partnering, and its likely responsiveness to the cultural changes required. An analysis and evaluation of this information will raise awareness of the need for change and the nature of partnering and its various forms. This greater awareness will allow the RSL to select the most appropriate form of partnering to adopt, its scope, the pace at which it could be safely and successfully introduced within the partner organisations, and to begin identifying the criteria for partner selection.

The need to be clear on strategic goals means that the decision whether or not to adopt strategic partnering should be made at the highest level within an RSL's organisation and that of its potential partners. A key factor that needs to be taken into account by senior managers in the RSL organisations, and their counterparts in their potential partners, is the amount of leverage or influence that their development programme generates in its supply systems. Leverage is a measure of the ability of a customer – the RSL in this case – to exercise control over resources in other organisations in its supply systems, and then to influence how those resources are managed in such a way that it becomes possible to appropriate greater value for itself.

The amount of leverage an RSL has will be determined by the total value and continuity of its development programme. If an RSL has a small and infrequent development programme then it will have little leverage over its suppliers, and the closeness of its relationships with its suppliers will be limited to project-specific partnering. If, however, an RSL has a significant and continuous flow of schemes it will have sufficient leverage to progress beyond project-specific partnering to some form of strategic partnering or alliance. If an RSL decides that it is possible to partner, and indeed that it would be advantageous to do so, it will need to set the policy and strategy for developing the kind of relationships that it wants with its suppliers.

The other vital aspect of partnering is the acceptance of the need for win–win thinking where all organisations involved receive appropriate rewards through increased mutual competitive advantage. Gaining acceptance of the need for mutual competitive advantage is a major factor in the successful implementation and operation of strategic partnering. For mutual competitive advantage to be truly effective, the members must collectively agree strategic goals for the whole of the supply chain. Traditionally, members of supply chains in all sectors of the economy have not shared with each other their strategic thinking in this way, and so gaining acceptance can be problematic. Given their pivotal role in their supply systems, RSLs need to acknowledge this and start the process of building mutual competitive advantage by being as precise as possible about their own policy, strategy and objectives, and the role that partnering is to play within their future business plans. They also need to recognise that their partners will have quite different business objectives from their own. This means that over time long- and short-term issues and different stakeholder interests will need to be taken into account, balanced and accommodated.

The need for planning and leadership

Early in developing its approach to partnering, Knightstone produced a plan for Egan compliance and other related issues such as partnering. This included developing a matrix identifying the actions required including identifying a partnering champion, preparing for and obtaining Construction Clients' Charter Status, training key personnel in the use of HQIs and KPIs, and developing new procurement guidance including new audit requirements and procedures to support more collaborative approaches. It also provided a programme for the implementation of their chosen approach.

Guinness formed a steering group to develop its partnering approach and promote it within its organisation. The membership of the group included a Group Director, a Development Strategy Manager, a Maintenance Strategy Manager, a Regional Surveyor, an Area Maintenance Surveyor and a Housing Manager.

The process of external and internal review will inform RSLs and their potential partners as to the most appropriate form of interorganisational relationships to develop. There are a number of options when choosing the type of partnering to be adopted, as explained in the ECI publication *Partnering in the Social Housing Sector*.

A Handbook. An RSL wishing to partner must first address the issue of what type of relationship it requires with its suppliers before electing to follow any particular form of partnering. The choice will be determined by a number of factors, including the type, volume and flow of work provided by the RSL and the attractiveness of the account to its potential partners. Other important factors are the planned duration and closeness of the relationship. In terms of duration there are two main choices: project-specific partnering and strategic partnering. In project-specific partnering the relationship is restricted to a single project, and the resulting benefits will also be limited. Strategic partnering is more ambitious, as the relationship is allowed to extend over a number of projects (known as a framework agreement) or a stated period of time (known as a term agreement). In this more advanced approach the benefits can be substantial. In terms of the closeness of the relationship, again there is a range of options, from arms-length transactions to a strategic alliance. A strategic alliance is the closest relationship short of a merger or a friendly takeover. It is used where a close relationship between the partners has been established over a number of partnering agreements and where they want to collaborate even more closely to maximise the use of each other's resources and further enhance mutual competitive advantage. This has been described as 'third-generation partnering'.

Figure 3.4 shows the wide range of relationships and contracts available to clients and their advisors when choosing their contracting strategy with main contractors and other key suppliers. The vertical axis shows the range of possible relationships from arms length through a number of increasingly closer and more collaborative relationships to a strategic alliance. The horizontal axis shows the range of contracts from a firm standard contract (modified to the benefit of the client, and to shift all risks to the contractor) through to a memorandum of understanding or an oral contract.

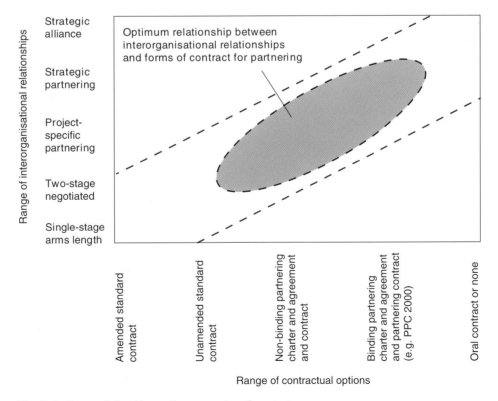

Fig. 3.4. Determining the optimum contracting strategy

The objective is to match the form of contract to the closeness and openness of the developing business relationship and the degree of competence trust that exists at that time. Where considerable confidence in the business relationship exists, and where there is a high level of competence trust between the parties, there will be less need for a firm contract. The robustness of the relationship between the RSL and the contractor should be continuously assessed during the development of the partnering relationship over a number of schemes. If the business relationship proves to be robust and beneficial to all parties, then alternative forms of contract can be used which more closely match the nature of the developing partnership, the degree of trust that exists between the parties, the allocation of risk, and their targets for performance improvement. An optimal contracting strategy for that particular partnering approach can be planned and implemented in an open and transparent way over a period of time that suits all the parties involved. In this way, the relationship gradually becomes more important in binding the parties together than a more formal contract.

The standard forms of building contracts are not an ideal basis for forging more collaborative customer–supplier relationships as they are closely associated with the adversarial relationships and lack of trust that traditionally have dogged the construction industry over many years. However, the role of the contract is often overemphasised in building partnering relationships. *Government Construction Procurement Guidance*, which is quoted in the SDS requirements, recommends the use of standard contracts with a framework agreement as the best means of setting up partnering arrangements. Partnering arrangements can be set up and implemented satisfactorily by combining one of the standard forms of contract with a partnering charter and agreement. The charter and agreement can set out the true understanding between the parties and the special factors in their relationships and projects. As confidence in the relationship develops, one of the partners may wish to move towards the use of one of the new more 'intelligent' and collaborative partnering contracts. These new contracts are drafted to be more conducive to partnering than the traditional forms of construction contract, and are less likely to be used as a weapon at times when the relationship comes under strain. Although these new contracts seek to more intelligently underpin the closer, more open and collaborative relationships associated with partnering there is still considerable nervousness about using them at this early stage in their development and use. For example, in PPC 2000, unless the constructor accepts full responsibility for the whole project, RSLs are concerned that they will be responsible for any failure by the 'core group' to coordinate the delivery of timely design information to the constructor. Furthermore, if there are any problems with the completed scheme, an RSL may face difficulties in trying to show which of the participants in the project are responsible for the problems.

These examples of the problems demonstrate how important it is that the partners have sufficient trust in each other's competence to perform (competence trust) in delivering scheme developments before using such contracts. Clearly, RSLs should seek legal advice before using a new partnering contract, and such advice should be taken from a lawyer who understands the principles and practice of partnering and has been fully briefed by the partners, and their partnering facilitator, on the openness, closeness, robustness and degree of trust in the business relationships within the partnership.

PPC 2000

Project Partnering Contract (PPC) 2000 emerged from the work of the Construction Industry Council Partnering Task Force.

It is based on the concept of the multiparty construction contract, where the key players are all involved with the project from an early date.

The parties to the contract are the contractor (referred to in the contract as the 'constructor') and the design team and any other consultants or specialists.

The original signatories form the partnering team and each partner appoints a representative to form a core group, which drives the project forward. The client appoints a client representative, who acts effectively as the contract administrator.

The PPC has been referred to as an 'intelligent' contract. An 'intelligent' contract is an expression of the genuine understanding between the parties and their real objectives. It provides a formal recognition and statement of their mutual interdependence without ignoring key issues and legitimate rights.

A recent survey of over 1000 individuals and 150 organisations undertaken by Masons solicitors showed that multiparty contracts such as PPC 2000 are not yet widely used. This may well indicate that industry is not yet sufficiently at ease with its partnering relationships to feel confident about using such a different form of contract.

The preferred forms of contract identified by the respondents to the survey are shown below:

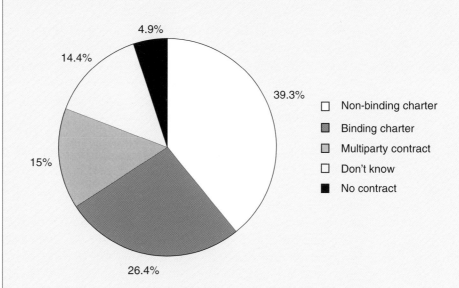

Trust

Trust is seen as more of an output of a relationship rather than an input, although some degree of trust must exist between the partners before they would contemplate embarking on partnering.

Three types of trust have been identified in supply chains:

O *contractual trust* – the mutual expectation that promises of a written or verbal nature will be kept;

O *competence trust* – the confidence that a trading partner is competent to carry out a specific task;

O *goodwill trust* – commitments from both parties that they will do more than is formally required.

Managing close customer–supplier relationships requires substantial investment. This means that RSLs should have closer relationships with only those suppliers that have the greatest impact on the success of their business and development projects. They should also choose their partnering approach according to the degree of fit between their respective competencies. The partners need to be aware that the required closeness of the relationship and the number of parties involved impact on how the relationships should be managed and the time and resources needed to build and sustain them. Although project-specific partnering could be seen as requiring the least investment in time and resources, this is not necessarily the case. The early steps in relationship building are often slow and resource-intensive as relationships and trust are painstakingly built. Also, considerable effort and investment will need to go into developing the necessary internal preparedness within the RSL's own organisation and engaging its people in the change process. In addition, rationalising the supplier base and choosing the most appropriate partners – even project-specific partners – is a vitally important aspect of early partnering and therefore a time-consuming and expensive process.

In the case of social housing the accountability of adopted arrangements and the nature of the relationships between the partners should be a prime policy consideration, and only those arrangements that are able to demonstrate the highest standards of propriety should be considered. The adopted partnering arrangements should be open, accountable and above reproach in all respects and should follow, as far as possible, the guidance set out in the Housing Corporation's SDS and *Partnering in the Social Housing Sector*, which is produced by the European Construction Institute. RSLs intending to adopt strategic partnering and framework agreements also need to ensure compliance with the relevant EU Procurement Directives.* A good partnering advisor or facilitator will be able to advise RSLs on this and other issues such as choosing the most appropriate form of partnering, assisting in building relationships, dealing with any misunderstandings and/or disagreements and setting up KPIs and other measurement systems. A lawyer should be consulted in relation to the use of the most appropriate form of contract and arrangements for the allocation of risk and the sharing of rewards.

As partnering is a challenging innovation, the policy and strategy should be realistic in terms of the up-front investment of resources needed, timescale, and the degree of responsiveness of the organisations involved to change. RSLs should be careful not to allow the development of unrealistic expectations in the early stages of implementation. As has already been explained, the experience of the BPiPG is that partnering should initially be adopted on an experimental basis in pilot projects. Introducing partnering on an experimental basis allows the approach to be reviewed, evaluated and modified or adapted before being introduced into an RSL's full programme of development schemes. The BPiPG also suggest that although the ultimate objective is to directly involve all the key stakeholders in the partnering

* In most cases these do not apply to RSLs as the EU Directives on procurement have a diminimus value of public subsidy of about £4 million and RSLs are not classed as public bodies. The Directives may apply if the contract involves the transfer of public assets (e.g. land) over £4 million in value and the percentage subsidy this represents is in excess of 50% – this scenario might occur on large-scale regeneration projects. EU Directives may also apply in the case of long-term strategic partnerships where the subsidy for a series of small projects may exceed this value. Legal advice should be sought if it is considered possible that EU Directives on procurement may apply.

approach, the pilot projects should initially be based on building relationships between the three key participants: RSLs and their first-tier suppliers – consultants and main contractors.

The BPiPG also used positioning matrices – based on the strategic competitive positioning model – to plan the implementation of their partnering approach in four main stages.

The strategic competitive positioning model

This model has been used by successful Japanese manufacturers to build mutual competitive advantage in a business environment. It shows the development stages an assembler and its supplier network needs to go through in order to retain and increase competitive advantage.

The benefits gained in each successive stage of the model are primarily the result of the collective learning by the participating organisations through their combined efforts at *kaizen*.

Part of a typical matrix for use in the social housing sector is shown below:

Element of the partnering approach	Stage 1: historical practice	Stage 2: 1999–2001	Stage 3: 2001–2004	Stage 4: 2004–2006
Relationship type and length	Adversarial and project by project	Project-specific partnering	Strategic partnering in a framework agreement	Strategic alliance
Form of contract	Standard Joint Contracts Tribunal (JCT) form of contract with amendments	Standard JCT unamended contract with non-binding charter and agreement	Partnering contract such as PPC 2000	Bespoke partnering contract
Number of first-tier suppliers	Long list of main contractors and consultants (first-tier suppliers)	Short list of three preferred main contractors and consultants (first-tier suppliers)	Two main contractors and consultants	Single sourcing – one main contractor and consultant
Scope of partnering in the supply chain	None	Partnership involving the RSL, consultant and main contractor	Partnership involving the RSL, consultant, main contractor and key specialist subcontractors and suppliers	Key participants in whole supply network
Quality	Minimal formal or systematic activity based on supervision by RSLs	KPIs, HQIs and quality assurance methodologies in place and applied by partners	Total quality management (TQM) and business excellence approaches being implemented by first-tier suppliers	KPIs, HQIs and quality assurance extended to key organisations in the whole supply network
Cost transparency	Low	Partly transparent in first-tier suppliers	Open-book accounting at first-tier level	Partly transparent in key areas of the whole network
Learning	Individual learning with some intraorganisational learning	Organisational and some interorganisational learning at the interfaces between partners in the first tier	Interorganisational learning involving key partners	Network learning

These matrices are made up of the characteristics of the changing relationship between RSLs, consultants, contractors and other partners as they seek to build mutual advantage. Using the matrix the partners can establish where they presently stand in developing their relationship and plan its future direction over an agreed time period.

3.5. The key actions to be taken by RSLs

These are presented as an implementation audit table.

RSL implementation audit table

Actions	By when	Specific actions required	What implementation looks like
Ensure full and visible commitment and support from your board and very senior management within your own organisation			
Be clear on the reasons why you are embarking on partnering, the rationale for the selected partnering approach and its objectives and criteria for success – certainty of the programme and cost, a given quality standard, minimum whole-life cost of ownership, sustainability (economic, social and environmental), improved health and safety, increased use of local labour, more respect for people, etc.			
Retrospectively measure the performance of recently completed development projects against the success criteria identified above to form benchmarks against which to measure the effectiveness of your partnering approach and demonstrate greater value and growing mutual competitive advantage			
Review your standing orders, financial regulations and administrative arrangements to ensure that they support partnering and the development of closer, longer-term and more collaborative relationships with your suppliers whilst providing similar safeguards and ensuring probity			
Talk to potential construction partners, tell them of your plans and incorporate as many of their views and ideas as you can into developing your policy and strategy for partnering			
Encourage and support learning and training about partnering, supply chain competition, more collaborative customer–supplier relationships, and continuous improvement within your organisation			
Appoint appropriate change leaders, champions and partnering advisors (from within and outside your organisation) within your own organisation and at the interfaces with your suppliers, local authorities and other stakeholders			
Consider setting up a partnering task force, steering group or stakeholder panel to help shape your partnering approach, select your partners, set your objectives, and drive it forward			
Choose the most appropriate form of partnering and contracts that best fit your circumstances and scheme developments			

RSL implementation audit table (contd)

Actions	By when	Specific actions required	What implementation looks like
Use positioning matrices to help you to draw up a partnering plan and a programme for its adoption and implementation			
Make clear to your own people your commitment to the changes associated with more collaborative supplier relationships, supply chain competition, continuous improvement and a total quality approach			
Make clear to your partners your commitment to closer and more collaborative customer–supplier relationships, supply chain management, continuous improvement and a quality-driven approach to procurement			
Make clear your commitment to reviewing, reshaping, coordinating and integrating your project processes and supply chains			
Encourage a fair supplier selection and payment regime by setting a good example in your relationships with your consultants and main contractor			
Be realistic in terms of what can be achieved, and reduce your risks by experimenting with project-specific partnering in pilot projects and avoiding single sourcing			
Keep your partnering approach as simple as possible. In the first instance restrict your approach to project-specific partnering and to your consultants and main contractors (first-tier suppliers) whilst requiring them to represent other major stakeholders such as tenants, management departments, local authorities, specialist and trade subcontractors, and suppliers			
Ensure customer focus by making sure that the needs of tenants, housing managers and operating departments are paramount in developing your partnering approach			
Be systematic in your approach by working on all elements of the partnering approach shown in Figure 3.2 and following the innovation cycle shown in Figure 3.1			
Make it clear to your partners that that nothing is forever and that your partnering approach will survive only as long as it continues to deliver mutual competitive advantage			
Recognise the need to gradually shift from specifying solutions through overly complex and prescriptive specifications to empowering your suppliers whilst continuing to define and communicate through performance specifications what constitutes best value for your tenants, development departments and housing managers			
Recognise that main contractors (particularly those who are developers in their own right) often have well-developed supply chains over which they already have considerable influence and ability to leverage value			
Explore the benefits to be gained by adopting the products and services from the main contractors' existing supply chains rather than using your own supply chains over which you may have limited leverage due to your more modest development programme. Recognise that the benefits can be particularly significant where a main contractor is also a major developer in its own right			

RSL implementation audit table (contd)

Actions	By when	Specific actions required	What implementation looks like
Seek to provide a more consistent approach to development to help build and sustain closer, more open and collaborative relationships, and encourage changes in behaviour within your own organisation and throughout your supply chains			
Ensure the appropriate level of commitment and allocation of resources to adopt, implement and sustain the partnering approach			
Involve your auditor as a stakeholder in the decision-making process on the type of partnering to be adopted and agree what audit information will be required, what form it should take and when it should be provided			

3.6. The key actions to be taken by consultants and contractors

Actions	By when	Specific actions required	What implementation looks like
Develop and demonstrate to RSLs your awareness, knowledge and understanding of their requirements and supply systems and your growing knowledge and understanding of partnering and supply chain management			
Talk to RSLs openly and constructively about partnering and supply chain management			
Encourage and help RSLs to develop realistic, yet stretching, approaches to partnering			
Help RSLs to collect the evidence to help them decide whether to partner, and which form of partnering to adopt			
Refocus your own policies and strategies and business objectives so that they synergistically integrate with those of RSLs			
Begin reshaping your own internal structures and processes and developing your people so that your organisation is more aligned with that of your key RSL clients			
Persuade potential RSL partners of the need for mutual competitive advantage and win–win business relationships if partnering is to be successful and sustainable			

3.7. The key barriers to be addressed

Key barriers	Proposed solutions
The negative impact of the uncertainties and inefficiencies – resulting from periodic changes in policy direction and levels of investment by the Housing Corporation and planning policies by local authorities – on an RSL's leverage in its supply chains	
Building the necessary internal and external commitment for genuine and sustainable partnering at all levels	
Deciding on the appropriate scope of the partnering approach, including the number of partners to involve and the length and closeness of the relationship	
Determining the appropriate pace of change by setting sufficiently stretching yet achievable targets for improvement	
Having the necessary confidence in the openness of relationships to embark on strategic partnering	
Having the right and effective performance measurement methods and historical benchmark data on which to justify the move to closer and more collaborative relationships	

Element 2. Leadership and diffusion

As can be seen from Figure 3.2, partnering, particularly in its most advanced forms, is increasingly being recognised as a challenging multidimensional innovation in procurement. This means that strong and effective leadership is vital in bringing about the substantial internal and external structural and attitudinal changes needed if it is to be successful. Leadership in this context comprises the processes by which individuals and organisations are empowered to work together in a closer and more collaborative way. This means that the leaders and champions of partnering need to believe in and be totally committed to the concept of more collaborative relationships and to driving it forward. By virtue of their position and influence in the development process, RSLs have a key role in spearheading change in the relationships between the main project participants and the way schemes are developed. In particular, senior managers in RSLs have a pivotal role to play by empowering others (within and outside their own organisation) to collective action by:

○ visibly demonstrating their commitment to the concept of partnering to generate greater collaboration and more integrated teams;
○ providing the appropriate front-end resourcing and assistance;
○ overcoming the resistance to cultural change within and between organisations;
○ developing a no-blame culture;
○ recognising and rewarding people's efforts and achievements in relation to partnering.

Leaders also need to work to close the gap that can often exist between their vision of partnering and interorganisational relationships and the reality of the resources currently available to them. Where their current resources, capabilities and ways of working are inadequate to meet these objectives they will need developing in order to meet the demands of the new approach. This implies preparing their people to do things differently and resourcefully and, in the case of the more advanced forms of partnering, to fundamentally rethink business relationships, organisational structures, processes, roles and responsibilities. Meeting these challenges means that leaders need to abandon much of the orthodoxy of conventional wisdom and current thinking and actively involve employees and partners in identifying issues and solving problems and creating new ways of working. Senior managers in RSLs can benchmark their progress in leading this change in their supply chains and increasing customer focus by reference to the Construction Clients' Charter Framework. In 2002, the National Housing Federation published a step-by-step guide to the charter called *Implementing the Clients' Charter*. This guide explains the philosophy and process behind becoming a chartered client including the significance of the charter in promoting cultural change in the construction industry and the leadership role of repeat clients, such as housing associations, in building effective partnerships. Seeking charter client status provides a means by which RSLs can prepare themselves internally for partnering and to take a more strategic approach in their relationships with their construction partners.

The Housing Corporation has made it a condition that RSLs which receive social housing grant (SHG) development funding must have client charter status. As part of their registration, RSLs must develop improvement plans which are reviewed by Achilles, a management consultancy organisation.

As well as needing 'visionary' leadership at the most senior levels, partnering also requires 'integration' and 'fulfilment' leaders at departmental and project levels, and at the interface between the partner organisations.

Construction Clients' Charter Framework

The charter provides for construction clients to commit themselves to effecting continuous improvements with measurement as its basis. It is primarily aimed at clients, what they should be doing and how they should be behaving to encourage improved performance from their construction projects and raising standards in the quality of their product.

The charter gives guidance on 'leadership' and 'focus on the customer' for clients in general and RSLs in particular. This includes:

O providing client leadership, both for improvement in procurement processes and for the supply side to develop and innovate to meet clients' needs;
O setting clearly defined and, where possible, quantified objectives and realistic targets for achieving these;
O fostering trust throughout the supply chain by treating suppliers fairly and ensuring a fair payment regime;
O promoting a team-based non-adversarial approach among clients, advisers and the supply chain;
O adopting a partnering approach wherever possible, with strategic partnering considered;
O identifying risk and how best to manage it;
O collecting and interpreting data on the performance in use of their construction solutions for the purposes of learning and feedback;
O promoting sustainability;
O standardisation and off-site assembly;
O respect for all.

The distributed leadership model

'Visionary' leader – director or senior executive
Typical leadership tasks:

O   mission statement;
O   vision and corporate values;
O   anticipate and respond to the external environment;
O   transform the organisation.

'Integration' leader – department head, regional director
Typical leadership tasks:

O   link business units into the mission and vision;
O   develop the organisation's systems, processes and infrastructure;
O   reconcile conflicting interests and goals between internal units;
O   develop and champion a strong collaborative culture;
O   innovate and share knowledge;
O   recruit and develop talent.

'Fulfilment' leader – project manager, supervisor
Typical leadership tasks:

O   please the customer/client;
O   deliver operating results on time;
O   uphold standards;
O   make continuous improvements;
O   unlock individual potential;
O   increase productive use of resources;
O   drive out waste.

Another key aspect of the leadership role is diffusion. This is the process by which leaders ensure that the ideas of partnering are spread to and assimilated by individuals and groups within the partner organisations and projects.

Diffusion

The diffusion process is concerned with how innovations are spread and assimilated within an organisation or cluster of organisations in a partnership, over a period of time. In other words, it is the spread of a new idea from its source to its ultimate users or adopters.

The speed with which a new idea is diffused or spread depends on:

O   the relative advantage of the new idea;
O   the degree to which the adopters or users of the new idea feels that it is consistent with their present needs, values and behaviour;
O   the degree to which the new idea is difficult to understand and use – more complex innovations take longer to diffuse;
O   the degree to which the new idea can be tried on a limited basis – the more opportunity to try, the easier it is for the adopters or users to evaluate;
O   the degree to which results from the use and ownership of the new idea are observable and describable to others, i.e. the ease of seeing the new idea's benefits and attributes.

The inclusion of diffusion in the model is an acknowledgement of the importance of gaining acceptance for, and understanding of, the partnering approach to be adopted throughout the partner organisations and their scheme developments. If the partnering is to be meaningful and sustainable, the changes associated with the model need to penetrate deep within the organisations and project teams involved. However, it is important to recognise that this diffusion process can take considerable time given the resistance to change that exists in many organisations. This is especially the case with a complex multifactor innovation, such as the advanced forms of partnering, with its strong emphasis on the need for changes in the softer aspects of relationship building such as individual and collective behaviour and attitudes. As this requires significant changes in culture, both cultural assimilation and adaptation are important factors to be addressed by the leaders and champions of partnering in the diffusion process. Cultural assimilation is the process through which individuals and groups are not only aware of the differences and nuances of a new culture but are also able to incorporate these differences into daily work. Cultural adaptation is the process through which individuals and groups become able to function successfully in a new culture. As well as promoting the innovation, once the innovation is underway, leaders and champions also have a key role to play in sustaining the partnering relationships so that they do not become complacent and uncompetitive and that they continue to add value through mutual competitive advantage.

3.8. The key actions to be taken by RSLs

These are presented below as an implementation audit table.

RSL implementation audit table

Actions	By when	Specific actions required	What implementation looks like
Recognise the significance of your leadership and diffusion role as an intelligent client at the core of the new scheme development process			
Assess the current effectiveness of your new scheme developments by using measures such as HQIs and KPIs, benchmark the results against other RSLs, and use the information to help draw up a business plan for partnering			
Work to increase the volume and continuity of your development programmes in order to increase your leverage in your supply chains and communicate your efforts to your own people and partners			
Use your leverage and influence to play a key role in leading the introduction of partnering into your new development of schemes by persuading potential partners to adopt an appropriate approach to partnering, increase openness and transparency, and embark on changing behaviour and attitudes to improve performance			

RSL implementation audit table (contd)

Actions	By when	Specific actions required	What implementation looks like
Constantly review your external environment to identify the need for change and to ensure that your developing approach to partnering remains focused on the appropriate priorities and objectives			
Constantly audit your own internal capabilities and those of your partners in relation to partnering and responsiveness to change			
Set up a task force, stakeholder panel, core or steering group to help you to shape and drive forward your partnering approach			
Appoint partnering champions who believe in, and are totally committed to, driving forward partnering, including making the necessary cultural, strategic and operational changes			
Prepare your champions of partnering for their role, place them in key areas within your own organisation, within projects and at the interface with partners, and give them clear guidance and visible encouragement, support, incentives and rewards			
Encourage your champions to measure performance, openly evaluate it, compare it with that of others within and outside the partnership and to use the knowledge to draw up a business plan to close the gap between procurement objectives and your current capabilities			
Empower all people within your own organisation and those of your partners to work together in a way that: O increases focus on the end user; O provides meaning and purpose to partnering; O develops a common goal or vision in terms of closer and more collaborative relationships; O focuses on the seven elements of the partnering model; O helps people feel less fearful and more confident about change; O ensures mutual benefits from partnering; O transforms relationships and processes			
Acknowledge that if partnering is to be successfully implemented and sustained it needs to be based on rewards for all the people and parties involved. Provide appropriate rewards, including maintaining or increasing margins for main contractors and their subcontractors and suppliers			
Ensure commitment and avoid complacency and cosy relationships by setting clear goals and stretching targets for improvement against HQIs, KPIs and other measures of performance, and then applying intense pressure on your own people and partners to meet those targets			

3.9. The key actions to be taken by consultants

Actions	By when	Specific actions required	What implementation looks like
Recognise your key leadership and supporting role in helping RSLs and their partners in adopting the appropriate business relationships and form of partnering			
Develop your own understanding of partnering, more collaborative interorganisational relationships and integrated teams			
Help senior top managers in RSLs and their development teams to adopt more collaborative and synergistic relationships and integrated processes with main contractors			
Help RSLs and their partners to assess the current performance of their scheme developments and develop more appropriate ways of measuring progress towards key performance targets			
Push for mutual competitive advantage by ensuring appropriate levels of profitability for contractors, specialist and trade subcontractors, and suppliers in return for their greater commitment to openness and transparency, cooperation, and continuous improvement against HQIs and KPIs			
Champion the quality of new development schemes and aim to maximise the economic, social and environmental sustainability of scheme developments			
Ensure that you understand environmental, economic and social sustainability and how they can be reconciled and implemented in the context of different social housing developments			
Understand the HQI system and be able to propose ways in which the supply chain can of improve scores while minimising cost			

3.10. The key actions to be taken by main contractors

Actions	By when	Specific actions required	What implementation looks like
Help RSLs and consultants to lead change in scheme developments and adopt more collaborative approaches to procurement			
Lead change in your own supply chains by using your own leverage and influence to align and stabilise downstream supply chains, develop longer-term relationships with specialist and trade subcontractors and suppliers, and negotiate greater value in exchange for more continuity of work, fairer payment and retention regimes, and more certain and higher profits			
Use your leverage and influence as developers to obtain sites and initiate scheme developments in order to maintain or increase the flow of work to the partners in the supply chain			

3.11. The key collective actions to be taken

Actions	By when	Specific actions required	What implementation looks like
Use your collective knowledge, understanding, leverage, influence and skills to adopt more collaborative approaches to scheme development, and encourage changes in culture to achieve continuous improvement throughout and between scheme developments and their supply chains			

3.12. The key barriers to be addressed

Key barriers	Proposed solutions
The lack of leverage and influence that many smaller RSLs have over their supply chains because of their small and intermittent development programmes	
The lack of leadership, involvement, commitment and understanding of enabling agencies and local authority planning departments upstream in the development process	
The lack of clear leadership and commitment to the partnering approach by any of the parties	
The lack of understanding of the diffusion process and the difficulties in overcoming the considerable barriers to cultural change	
Building sufficient confidence in partnering and trust in the intra- and interorganisational relationships so that all transactions and processes become more open and transparent	
The lack of leadership by main contractors in extending the approach downstream to involve specialist and trade subcontractors and suppliers	

Element 3. Setting up, developing and sustaining a balanced set of relationships

As has been argued earlier in this report, there is now considerable evidence, from other industries and other sectors of the construction industry, of the technical and commercial value of developing longer-term and more collaborative customer–supplier relationships. Such relationships developed over several projects rather than a single project can create the environment needed for continuous improvement to reduce costs, add value for the end user, and suitably reward suppliers for their efforts. Longer-term relationships also offer ways of working together more closely so that the skills and knowledge throughout the partnership can be brought together and focused on continuously improving product design, buildability, functionality, maintainability, and ways of working, whilst maintaining or indeed increasing margins for suppliers.

The benefits of longer-term relationships

Research undertaken by the Reading Construction Forum indicates that project-specific partnering can result in single-figure savings. However, where partnering is used over a series of projects 30% savings are common, and a 50% reduction in cost and an 80% reduction in time are possible in some cases.

As RSLs move to longer-term and more collaborative relationships with fewer other parties, choosing the most appropriate partners becomes an even more significant factor in the success of their development projects. However, there are significant concerns associated with this approach, including the existing and future volume of work and cash flows from RSLs. A further concern relates to building the necessary degree of common interest and trust that, over a period of time, will persuade the parties to forgo opportunistic behaviour. There are also understandable concerns relating to the dangers of the development of cosy relationships and uncompetitive costs and practices.

A major dilemma to be faced by RSLs in relation to maintaining their competitive position is whether to adopt single or multiple sourcing. If an RSL decides to allocate all its development work to one consultant and one contractor it will clearly maximise its leverage over them. This could result in a better and more economic service than if it was to divide its work, and hence its leverage or influence, between two or more suppliers. However, if it decides to choose a single main consultant and contractor it is in effect creating monopolistic sources. If, on the other hand, the RSL uses, say, three preferred contractors and consultants it will maintain competitive forces through intersupplier rivalry to find a favoured position in the partnership, but will dissipate its purchasing power and leverage. This is a particular problem for RSLs with small or medium-sized development programmes. The main advantages associated with each approach are outlined below.

The advantages of single sourcing to the RSL include:

○ the RSL is likely to have more leverage over its consultant and main contractor;
○ the consultant and contractor ought to be able to offer a price advantage because of the economies of scale and the reduction of tendering and transaction costs;
○ personal relationships can be more easily established and maintained, thus making communications more open and effective;
○ these closer relationships can, over a period of time, result in greater and more focused mutual effort to reduce cost and add value;
○ more of the consultant's and main contractor's assets are likely to be made available and dedicated to the RSL – this is known as asset specificity;
○ designs, specifications, processes and methods of working are more easily standardised, integrated and improved;
○ monitoring and benchmarking of time, quality and other performance criteria are made easier.

The advantages of multiple sourcing include:

○ insurance against failure of the one main consultant and contractor;
○ a competitive environment can be maintained so that no one consultant or main contractor can afford to become complacent;

○ the RSL is protected against the dangers of a monopoly;
○ fewer moral responsibilities in the relationships between the RSL, the consultants and the main contractors should one of the partners wish to withdraw from the relationship at a later date;
○ increased flexibility in case of an increase or decrease in the RSL's development work;
○ scope for specialisms within preferred suppliers (e.g. with four preferred consultants and contractors, two could focus on refurbishment or maintenance work and two on new build, or two on urban regeneration and two on green field development – depending on the nature of the RSL's scheme developments).

Experience from other sectors of construction suggests that multiple sourcing is preferable – especially in the early stages of partnering where clients are not experienced at selecting partners on a long-term basis. Assuming that multiple sourcing is considered to be the most appropriate for most RSLs, then a process for selecting, say, four preferred consultants and main contractors can be envisaged as in Figure 3.5.

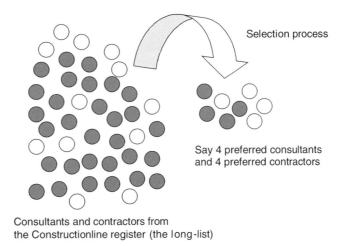

Selection process

Say 4 preferred consultants and 4 preferred contractors

Consultants and contractors from the Constructionline register (the long-list)

Fig. 3.5. Selection of preferred partners in a multiple-sourcing approach

Partner selection for longer-term relationships is complicated by the need to assess future as well as present capabilities. Present criteria to evaluate the performance of contractors often include the quality of products and services, cost predictability, time predictability, resources, the health and safety record, financial stability, and experience and expertise. In longer-term relationships, the RSL needs to be as clear as possible as to its development policies and strategies and the issues that need to be addressed in the context within which its future schemes are to be developed. The factors that can be significant in supplier selection and for assessing their subsequent performance can include:

○ the quality of their strategic leadership;
○ their emphasis on the primacy of total quality management and continuous improvement;
○ their willingness to work collaboratively and synergistically as partners;

○ their understanding of RSL objectives, culture, and the regulatory and funding regimes under which they have to operate;

○ their understanding of the determinants of functionality in social housing schemes;

○ their understanding of the complexity of urban regeneration schemes and how complex issues such as security and employment can be addressed;

○ their acceptance of the need for innovation and change and proactivity of thinking;

○ their openness and willingness to share information and knowledge;

○ the effectiveness of their strategic, operational and project planning;

○ their ability to manage risk and value, anticipate problems and generate solutions;

○ their ability to innovate to develop schemes that meet social, environmental and economic sustainability objectives;

○ their ability to manage supply chains and help unlock the potential of specialist and trade subcontractors and suppliers;

○ their ability to build competence trust and, later, goodwill trust in relationships.

The weightings for each of these factors will vary depending on the context within which individual RSLs and their supply systems operate. For RSLs operating in urban regeneration areas the social factors will be of major importance, whereas in rural areas environmental sustainability factors will be likely to dominate. The weightings given to these factors in partner selection can be determined by the steering group or task force charged with leading the RSL's partnering approach. These weightings should be made clear to prospective partners at the start of the selection process.

There are a number of mechanisms that RSLs can use to begin rationalising their supplier base and choosing their preferred consultants and main contractors for longer-term relationships. One such mechanism is to undertake retrospective assessments of the performance of consultants and contractors employed on previous schemes but measured against the new quality and partnering criteria outlined above. Alongside this, a 'quality questionnaire' can be prepared which should reflect what is expected of suppliers in the new customer–supplier relationships. Potential partners can then be asked to complete the 'quality questionnaire' as part of the selection process to help assess their capabilities. It can be helpful to all parties if this is done in the context of a pilot project but on the clear understanding that this could lead to a longer-term relationship in a framework or term agreement.

Typical questions asked of potential partners in a 'quality questionnaire'

○ How would you envisage maximising HQIs whilst keeping costs down to achieve best value?

○ How would you approach minimising running costs for tenants of completed housing schemes?

○ How would you go about ensuring completed dwellings are as flexible as possible to meet changing family composition whilst retaining the robustness of current technological solutions?

○ What methodology would you bring to determining the whole-life costs of schemes?

○ How would you apply continuous improvement tools and techniques in a longer-term relationship?

○ How would you go about maximising the economic benefit of schemes to the local area through the use of local labour and services?

Another required mechanism for selecting the most appropriate partners is to interview key personnel in the partner organisations, especially those individuals who will be part of the interface structures between the partner organisations and the RSL. In the case of selecting partners for a long-term strategic partnership, it may be worth investing the extra time and resources needed to hold these interviews at their offices and/or other facilities rather than those of the RSL. This can provide further useful insights into their culture and their ability to partner. In order to reduce the risk of choosing the wrong partners, RSLs with significant development programmes and leverage may wish to extend the decision-making process over a period of time and a number of projects. An initial selection of, say, four or five preferred suppliers can, over a period of time, and on the basis of their performance as partners on schemes, be reduced to, say, three. If considered advantageous this process of rationalisation can continue until the RSL is partnering with a single consultant and main contractor – a single-source supply. In this way, RSLs can gradually reduce their supplier base on the basis of demonstrable improvements in performance over a period of time. In turn, this approach will help the better suppliers to:

○ further differentiate themselves from their competitors;
○ reduce their substitutability and increase their indispensability;
○ provide greater continuity of work for themselves and their supply chains;
○ increase their organisational learning;
○ increase their reputation and justify their 'badging' as a 'partnering' contractor or consultant;
○ increase their profitability.

In the selection processes outlined above, the steering group or task force should be seeking out tangible and robust evidence that the supplier has the capabilities to be an effective long-term partner. This should include practical examples of how the supplier has addressed complex problems in the past and how they propose to help the RSL meet their future development objectives.

EU rules of procurement

There are some circumstances where EU rules may apply in initiating partner relationships and appointing consultants and main contractors under EU rules of procurement. The types of procedure available are 'open', 'restricted' and 'negotiated' procedures. As the open procedure can lead to an excessive number of tenders it is not recommended. The restricted procedure allows the number of organisations that may submit tenders to be restricted using a selection process in advance of tender invitation. The negotiated procedure takes two forms: 'competitive' and 'without a call for competition'. The 'competitive' approach enables RSLs, subject to certain regulations, to negotiate the terms of the contract with selected bidders, and may include a formal tender stage prior to negotiation. The 'without a call for competition' procedure is applicable only in the most exceptional circumstances. The restricted and competitive negotiated procedures are the recommended routes in all but exceptional circumstances. The method of restricted competition on the basis of partnering criteria and price has much to commend it in the context of the social housing sector, where public money is involved and which is governed by regulations that require transparency in precontractual and contractual relationships. The selection process for this method is described in *Government Construction Procurement Guidance*, Guidance No. 3, *Appointment of Consultants and Contractors*, which is available from the Office of Government Commerce.

As has already been stated, the process for the selection of consultants and main contractors can be conducted by the steering group or task force for partnering set up by the RSL. The panel can be used to establish the selection criteria, their weightings and thresholds, and the mechanisms by which partners will be selected for preferred supplier status. It should be innovative in how it goes about obtaining expressions of interest. For instance, it might invite end users, consultants, contractors and suppliers to participate in an informal seminar to outline its initial thinking, needs, opportunities, openness and receptiveness to ideas and to capture the views and ideas of end users and suppliers. Advertisements inviting companies to participate in such exploratory discussions are not subject to EU Procurement Directives. The RSL should make it clear that, in due course, invitations to bid to be partners will be requested, with companies being selected via an objective quality-based evaluation process. The feedback from the seminar will help the RSL's stakeholder panel to shape its approach to partner selection, the criteria to be used, and the method of selection.

The panel can then invite formal expressions of interest to partner from consultants and contractors registered on Constructionline (the long list) and from this, and its review of existing supplier performance, could draw up a short list of around five or six consultants and contractors who are formally invited to tender to be a partner. Guidance provided by the Office of Government Commerce, Guidance No. , *Appointment of Consultants and Contractors*, suggests that the selection criteria is based on information concerning the attributes of the tenderers under the headings of 'personal position' and 'economic and financial standing' (both met through registration on Constructionline) and 'technical capacity'. Technical capacity relates to resources, quality management and technical suitability for the RSL's pilot partnering project and subsequent projects under a framework or term agreement. The criteria listed under 'technical capacity' must be capable of being scored and audited. The relative importance allocated to each of the criteria can be established by giving it a percentage weighting.

As argued earlier, there are a number of factors to be taken into account in supplier selection in the context of longer-term customer–supplier relationships. These include the equality of mutual negotiating positions. Although an RSL may like to partner with one of its suppliers, this may not always be feasible because of inequalities in size or a lack of collaborative capability. An RSL with a small and infrequent development programme is likely to find it difficult to partner with a large main contractor and developer as it will be unlikely to have any significant influence on the way that the contractor operates. An RSL in this situation might find it more appropriate to partner with a smaller contractor that would find even its small and fragmented development programme attractive and hence be more responsive to the needs and aspirations of the RSL. However, smaller contractors are less likely to have the strategic thinking and management capacity to implement partnering and build mutual advantage. Alternatively, the RSL could collaborate with another RSL or RSLs to increase leverage by merging their development programmes.

Another factor is the geographical distribution of the RSLs existing and proposed housing stock. Major contractors can operate on a regional or national basis. Small contractors tend to operate locally. Similarly, subcontractors often operate on a subregional basis. This means that although it may be possible for RSLs with a wide spatial spread of scheme developments to build long-term relationships with national contractors, it is likely to be more problematic in the case of smaller contractors and subcontractors.

Once the partners have been selected, the relationship-building process in the partnership is often initiated by a strategy meeting attended by the most senior personnel of the participating organisations. It can be helpful if this is meeting is led by an independent trained facilitator. This strategy meeting should be the first of a series of meetings and workshops to help build the relationship and develop a more collaborative culture at the interface between the organisations.

Strategy meeting

The agenda for the strategy meeting could include:

O   an overview of how the partnership is to be established and its objectives and scope;

O   a confirmation of the contracting strategy (with either a standard contract with a partnering charter and agreement or a partnering contract);

O   targets for workload, performance improvement to add value, and mutual competitive advantage;

O   the continuous improvement methodologies and tools to be used;

O   the mechanisms for achieving the culture change including workshops, collective learning and external facilitation;

O   interface structures to be developed including allocation of staff, leaders and champions and the channels for information and physical flows;

O   an agreement on the procedures for dispute avoidance;

O   mechanisms for the diffusion of the partnering approach within the participating organisations;

It needs to be recognised that developing closer customer–supplier relationships also implies a power play when risks have to be allocated and the fruits of the increased competitiveness of the supply chain are shared. In this process, the share of risk and rewards allocated to each partner depends on its bargaining power, which is largely derived from its competencies and its position and influence in the development process and its supply chains. Conflicts can arise over the reallocation of risks and the sharing of rewards, and could inhibit the development of more collaborative relationships. As disputes are to be expected in a partnership, as in any relationship, the issue is not to try and avoid them but how to resolve them by agreeing general rules in advance. It is also important to recognise that conflicts are likely in the early days of the partnership when trust between the partners may still be limited and when there is still considerable uncertainty regarding the exact nature of the relationship being developed. Also at this time the partners will be grappling with the considerable challenges in making the shift from price-competitive customer–supplier relationships to a quality-based approach. During this process it is likely that the true capabilities of all the partners will begin to be revealed. It is important that this inevitable revelation of the true performance of all the partners is conducted in a no-blame culture and that any conflicts arising are dealt with positively and constructively and in a way that does not weaken the relationship but is instead used to strengthen it.

Conflict management procedure

A conflict management procedure is a methodology that can be helpful in resolving issues in the building of the relationship or specific scheme developments positively and constructively without resorting to mediation, adjudication, arbitration or the courts. It also provides a further way in which the partners can begin to understand each other, identify where power and knowledge resides and how decisions are made – all of which adds to mutual understanding.

A conflict management procedure works through a 'resolution ladder', which identifies the level at which disputes can arise and where they are to be resolved. Any issue that cannot be resolved at the lowest level of the 'resolution ladder' is referred to the next level of the ladder for its resolution. If it cannot be resolved at this level it is then automatically elevated to the next identified level on the ladder, and so on, until it is resolved. Prior to a dispute being referred up to the next level, the facts of the dispute are recorded, giving both sides' view, and the time allocated for resolving the dispute at that level, and in total, is agreed.

Once initiated, the partnership will need sustaining, which means it is necessary to establish a supportive and creative environment to support the people in the relationship. The people at the interface between the partners will need clear and regular confirmation of the continuing commitment and support of their senior management. The ongoing involvement of senior management will help to ensure collective strategy development and that the strategic goals of the partnership and the means of attaining them remain relevant and the main focus of the relationship. Regular meetings and workshops are needed to ensure open communication, win–win thinking and that individuals and groups remain focused on what is truly important in building the partnership. Such meetings are also vital in providing feedback on performance, identifying areas for improvement, and celebrating success.

Although building closer more collaborative relationships is important in partnering, it should be recognised that such relationships are only a means to an end – to continuously improve performance to add value and increase mutual competitive advantage. This means that having appropriate performance measures is a vital element in ensuring the developing relationship remains focused on these core objectives. The report *Rethinking Construction* makes a strong case for ambitious targets and effective measurement in improving performance. Such performance measures need to be explicit and mutually agreed, and the costs and benefits shared appropriately. Also, clear channels of communication should be established and defined to facilitate the effective flow of information in relation to performance measures and their effectiveness. This is a challenging agenda for the partners, and it can be helpful to appoint an outside independent consultant, relationship facilitator or partnering advisor to help overcome the resistance to cultural change and to support the development of the relationship and to monitor and benchmark its effectiveness.

While closer relationships can, in the longer-term, foster greater synergy, understanding and mutual trust, it must be recognised that they are not always appropriate. It is likely to remain more beneficial if a number of the more basic and/or one-off products and services required by RSLs continue to be procured on a price-competitive basis in arms-length relationships. Developing closer customer–

supplier relationships demands considerable investments in time and resources, and also involves considerable risks. Some of these include:

O the possible loss of long-term competitiveness of partners and the development of mutual overdependencies;

O the possible loss of flexibility, particularly in responding to sudden and substantial technological or organisational changes, as a close relationship with a selected supplier might restrict the RSL's access to new technology or methods of working;

O the dangers of selecting the wrong partners who lack the motivation and skills for future compatible collaborative capabilities;

O the difficulty of achieving balanced mutual bargaining positions and the appropriate governance of the partnership;

O the difficulties of maintaining sufficient and continuous development work to fully develop and sustain strategic partnering.

Where the RSL is adopting multiple sourcing, the award process to a specific scheme development, shown in Figure 3.6, can be seen as distinct from the selection process described above.

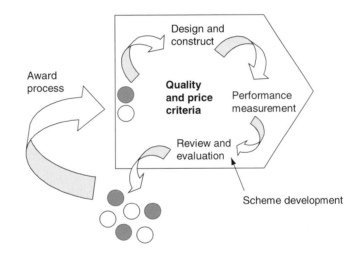

Fig. 3.6. *Award process for preferred consultants and contractors in a multi-sourcing approach*

The award process to a specific scheme should be conducted by a stakeholder panel that comprises the members of the steering group or task force, but augmented by the housing manager, the development manager, a tenant representative, and the maintenance manager for that particular development scheme. Other members might include the RSL's auditor, local authority officers, councillors and community representatives, and local people with commercial interests. In this way, continuity of the RSL's partnering policy is maintained between the overall strategy of the partnering steering group or task force and the stakeholder panels for specific schemes that are suitable for partnering. Whereas the selection process outlined earlier looked at the status and performance of potential partners, the award process aims to appoint the most appropriate consultant and contractor partners for a specific development scheme, and must be on the basis of best value for money for that project.

The RSL and its stakeholder panel will want to select those suppliers with the greatest experience and ability to satisfy the requirements and achieve the objectives of the specific development scheme. The key function of the stakeholder panel is to determine the scheme's objectives and communicate them to the project team. It also has an important role in reviewing the scheme at various stages to assess the extent to which these objectives are being met by the project team. The stakeholder panel should not contain any of the potential partners for the scheme, including consultants, because of possible conflicts of interest.

The award criteria must be appropriate, specific to the particular project, and relevant to assessing whether the bids from the preferred consultants and main contractors provide value for money. The criteria should focus on:

○ effectiveness in meeting the economic, social and environmental sustainability requirements for the particular project;
○ aesthetic and functional characteristics, such as design, operating costs, ease of use and adaptability of use, degree of innovation in product and process, maintainability and whole-life costs;
○ proposed HQI and KPI target scores and the means of achieving them;
○ proposals for managing the project such as procedures for planning, programming and management; risk identification and proposals for their management; and quality and health and safety plans;
○ the proposed project team and its organisation;
○ the technical suitability of the team for the project;
○ quality of services provided from external sources.

The stakeholder panel sets and communicates the objectives of the scheme and any threshold requirements for the project as a whole. The objectives for the scheme reflect what is valuable to the client, end users and other key stakeholders. These objectives may be categorised as scheme-specific (e.g. retention of a shop unit); valuable to the finished project (e.g. low fuel consumption); or valuable to the construction process (e.g. reduction of defects). The objectives should address sustainability in the following key areas:

○ *Environmental*. For example, low CO_2 emissions, high fuel efficiency in use and in construction, high water efficiency, minimum use of harmful products (CFCs, HFCs and treated timber), maximum use of renewable materials, maximum use of recyclable materials, and encouragement of reductions in car use and the 'green' behaviour of residents.
○ *Economic*. For example, maximum training opportunities, minimum running costs to allow tenants to maximise their incomes, maximum use of local small and medium enterprises (SMEs), maximum public transport opportunities to places of work, maximum use of local labour, maximum use of black-led contractors, maximum use of skills assessment/badging, minimum maintenance costs, and minimum capital costs.
○ *Social*. For example, defensible space, internal and external aesthetics, safety-enhanced environment (traffic, pedestrians and children), maximum planting, provision of safe and sustainable play areas, and maximum flexibility of individual dwellings for changing family requirements.

These criteria may, of course, overlap, as in the case of low running costs and low CO_2 emissions.

The RSL and its stakeholder panel will establish the hierarchy of value of each criterion and will weight their relative importance as percentages. For example: health and safety, 2%; innovation, 5%; defects, 8%; and 'green' credentials, 4%. The RSL and its stakeholder panel may also set scheme 'thresholds'. For example, the existing shop on the site is to be retained or the scheme does not proceed. There also may be thresholds within each of the quality criteria. For example, health and safety may have a weighting of 65%. This means that if the submission contained a score below this then the tender could be disqualified.

The scheme's objectives must be transformed into a contractor's proposal or tender, which under HM Treasury Guidance must be a 'quality' and 'price' tender. The quality proposal or tender should consist of a list of questions in relation to issues pertinent to the scheme and derived from the project objectives. It is aimed at selecting the contractor that is best equipped and motivated to satisfying the criteria for the particular scheme.

When the stakeholder panel undertakes the analysis of the contractor's proposal or tender against the scheme's objectives and criteria it is important that the decision-making and outcomes are carefully recorded for scrutiny by an auditor and to provide effective feedback to those involved as part of the partners' ongoing commitment to learning and performance improvement.

Once the successful project team has been formed they, and their supply chains, work up the project together. Their completed proposal is then referred back to the stakeholder panel for assessment against the scheme's objectives. The stakeholder panel then decides whether to go ahead with the project or to close it down. If the project is judged to be viable and good value, then a bid is submitted to the Housing Corporation and/or other funding agencies. Following success in obtaining funding, the RSL and the stakeholder panel make the decision to invest. The purchase of the site can go ahead, and the parties enter into contracts. The scheme is then implemented and the project team work together collaboratively, within the spirit and objectives of their partnership, to achieve the scheme's objectives. After completion, the project team undertakes a formal postconstruction review and shares its outcomes with the stakeholder panel and the RSL's partnering steering group or task group, so that an overall review of the project and the effectiveness of the partnership can be undertaken. The RSL, the stakeholder panel and the steering group or task force can then continue monitoring the effectiveness of the scheme in use and benchmarking it against other schemes by the RSL and its partners and partnered schemes by other RSLs.

3.13. The key actions to be taken by RSLs

These are presented as an implementation audit table.

RSL implementation audit table

Actions	By when	Specific actions required	What implementation looks like
Be clear about what it is you are looking for from your suppliers in your new customer–supplier relationshipsgiven the likely volume and continuity of your development schemes			
Using the vertical axis of Figure 3.4, decide on the most appropriate relationships with your key consultants and main contractors in the range from arms length to strategic alliance			
Make it clear to your own people and your partners why the new relationships are being developed			
Use Figure 3.4 to select and develop an appropriate contracting strategy that matches the form of contract (from amended standard forms of contract to an oral agreement) to the new relationship (from arms length to strategic alliance) with your partners			
Be innovative in how you go about understanding your supplier base of consultants and main contractors and selecting the most appropriate first-tier suppliers for your partnering approach			
Make sure that your approach complies with EU rules of procurement where they apply			
Set up a panel (e.g. your partnering steering group or task force) that will command the confidence of your Board and bidders to conduct the partner selection process. Make sure it has the appropriate mix of expertise, experience and understanding of your objectives and proposed approach to partnering			
The panel to decide on the criteria for partner selection and how their bids will be assessed			
The panel to actively and imaginatively seek out partners with the necessary culture, knowledge and competencies to enhance and complement your own internal capabilities within your partnering approach			
Make sure that the panel members meet and talk with the people who will actually be part of the team you allocate to your projects			
The panel to make it clear to tenderers in advance how they will be evaluated and the weightings you will be applying to the selection criteria, including any thresholds. The criteria to be made as objective and numerical as possible			
Decide and make clear to tenderers whether you intend to use single or multiple sourcing			
Don't change anything during the selection process			
Develop standard methods and documentation for the appraisal of tenderers			
Don't be taken in by the standard of prose or presentation skills of tenderers			
Focus on choosing partners with compatible collaborative capabilities and mutual bargaining positions			
Fully record the evaluation and selection process to demonstrate probity and value for money			

RSL implementation audit table (contd)

Actions	By when	Specific actions required	What implementation looks like
Provide feedback to the unsuccessful tenderers			
Organise a strategy meeting with your partners to start implementing the partnering approach			
Ensure mechanisms exist to support open and ongoing communication between the partners in order to develop and sustain the relationship			

3.14. The key actions to be taken by consultants

Actions	By when	Specific actions required	What implementation looks like
Refocus your role on to promoting, facilitating, supporting and sustaining the closer, more open and collaborative relationship between RSLs and main contractors, in a way that demonstrates added value and increased mutual advantage, rather than just advising RSLs and protecting their interests			
Help manage the project process so that key participants are involved at the appropriate time and fully engaged in the decision-making process			
Ensure that risks are identified, apportioned and managed, and gains shared, in a way that competence and goodwill trust are developed			
Help develop appropriate performance measures to drive the new relationship and monitor its effectiveness			
Collect and analyse the data from the HQIs, KPIs and other agreed performance measures in order to build the confidence of RSLs and main contractors in the new relationship, particularly in terms of value for money, the equitable allocation of risk, the appropriateness and fairness of profit margins, and the sharing of rewards			
Help develop 'improvement curves', 'radar diagrams' and other methods to graphically present past and present performance and negotiate targets for future improvement			
Use relationships with your other clients and main contractors to benchmark the performance of the partnership (using HQIs, KPIs and other performance measures) against the performance of other clients and main contractors in the social housing and other construction sectors			
Help the partners to move from the current focus on capital costs to the whole-life or total cost of ownership for RSLs			
Collect the evidence needed to decide whether appropriate relationships, processes and procedures are in place, that they have been properly implemented and gauge their effectiveness			
Collect the necessary evidence to verify whether value and mutual competitive advantage is being added as a result of the partnering arrangements			

3.15. The key actions to be taken by main contractors

Actions	By when	Specific actions required	What implementation looks like
Respond appropriately to the RSL's approach by ensuring the openness and transparency in the way in which you monitor your own performance and the performance of your supply chains matches the closeness and duration of the relationship offered by the RSL			
Match the principles of your relationships with RSLs and consultants in your relationships downstream with your key specialist and trade subcontractors and suppliers			
Use your own greater leverage as the result of the continuity of work and fairer treatment by your RSL partners to encourage change and performance improvements within your own organisation and your subcontractors and suppliers			

3.16. The key collective actions to be taken

Actions	By when	Specific actions required	What implementation looks like
Work to create an environment conducive to the process of building closer, more open and collaborative relationships aimed at increasing trust, adding value and increasing mutual competitive advantage			
Set up mechanisms to constructively resolve conflicts and deal with any unforeseen events, set-backs, barriers and problems in the adoption and implementation of partnering so that problems actually help to build relationships, improve understanding and increase people satisfaction			
Communicate regularly to exchange views, ideas, benefits and concerns, and report openly, transparently and honestly on progress and the difficulties and barriers to be addressed			
Appoint an independent outside consultant who has no other role in the project other than to act as a partnering facilitator and advisor			

3.17. The key barriers to be addressed

Key barriers	Proposed solutions
The traditional and deeply embedded adversarial relationships in construction supply chains, resulting from years of price-competitive tendering and reliance on firm contracts	
The current lack of transparency in relation to performance often found in traditional procurement approaches, development schemes and supply chains	
The present limited confidence in partnering as an effective innovation, the lack of trust in relationships and the likely continuance of opportunistic behaviour	
Difficulties of developing long-term, more collaborative relationships within the limitations of project-specific partnering and the relatively short duration of typical one-off scheme developments	
Difficulties of making the shift from project-specific partnering to strategic partnering	

Element 4. Integrating business, project and supply chain processes

For many years the lack of integration between the design and construction stages of projects has been seen as a major weakness of the construction process. Although main contractors and specialist and trade subcontractors understand price, few understand cost. In the present system the RSL specifies and the main contractor prices, then the main contractor specifies and then the trade and specialist contractors price, and so on down the supply chain. In partnering, the main contractor and the key specialist and trade subcontractors should be involved as early, and as much as possible, in the design, specification and costing of the scheme. The aim is to break out of the traditional sequential and highly fragmented development process and address the lack of integration between design, construction, operation and maintenance phases of housing schemes. In other words, the partners set out to design and cost the scheme, and plan its construction and subsequent operation simultaneously right from the beginning. This allows the partners to exploit the greater scope for change and innovation during the early stages of scheme developments, and is illustrated in Figure 3.7.

Strategic partnering in a framework or term agreement goes even further by providing the opportunity for main contractors and key subcontractors and suppliers to engage with RSLs and their scheme developments in an ongoing way. This provides the maximum opportunities for key suppliers to constantly work alongside RSLs and their consultants throughout all the stages of scheme developments and into their subsequent use, management and maintenance. The partners can work together in the all stages of schemes to apply value analysis, management and engineering techniques. This is illustrated in Figure 3.8.

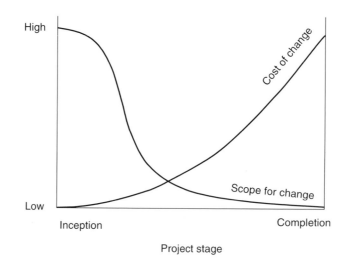

Fig. 3.7. *Relationship between scope for change and cost through the development process*

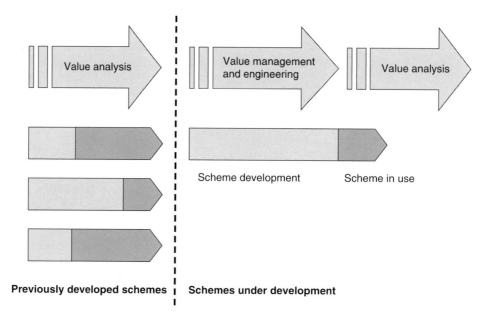

Fig. 3.8. *Applying value management in strategic partnering*

More recently, construction has also been encouraged to emulate practices from other industries by integrating project processes more closely with supply chain processes, as shown in Figure 3.9.

Customers in other industries have demonstrated the benefits of keeping their supply chains together and working alongside them over much longer periods of time than those normally associated with one-off construction projects. The scope for this ongoing integration and coordination is strongly dependent on the closeness and duration of the relationship between the parties, the structure of the supply system and the interface structures which have been set up to manage them on a day-to-day basis. Therefore, developing a balanced set of relationships, structuring and stabilising

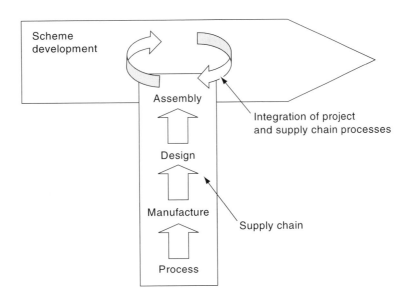

Fig. 3.9. *Integration of project and supply chain processes*

the supply system, integrating processes, and setting up the right interface structure to support them are seen as mutually reinforcing elements of the BPiPG's approach.

There are a number of possible ways to structure the interface between the partners in a construction project and to integrate project and supply chain relationships and processes. The project structure is the traditional and currently predominant interface structure in construction. A project is commonly defined as a non-repetitive activity that has a number of characteristics:

O it is goal oriented;
O it has a clear beginning and end;
O it has a particular set of constraints – usually centred on time and resources;
O the output of the project is measurable;
O something has been changed through the project being carried out;
O its relationships and processes are transient and temporary.

The management of projects involves planning, organising, directing and controlling activities in addition to motivating what is usually the most expensive resource on the project – the people. Planning involves deciding what has to be done, when and by whom. The resources need to be organised through activities such as procurement and recruitment. Directing activities towards a coherent objective within a temporary and transient organisational structure is a major management role. The activities also need controlling to ensure that they fit within the limits set for them at the start of the project.

The constant breaking up and remixing of project teams that characterises much of construction, coupled with its adversarial and contractual relationships, is not conducive to the integration of the sets of resources that exist in the project and the organisation. For effective projects the resources within organisations need to be mobilised to support projects and for organisations to be successful they need to feed back their experiences of projects into their business processes. The more advanced forms of partnering generate the long-term and closer relationships that can allow the better integration of these two sets of resources. Once the duration of the relationship between RSLs and their suppliers extends beyond the single project into a programme of projects – or framework agreement – then the partners can consider alternative supply chain and interface structures to achieve maximum integration of the resources in each of the partnering organisations. The pyramid offers an interorganisational structure that has been used with more stable supplier bases in other industries and, indeed, in some other construction sectors. Such a pyramid, demonstrating the tiers within the supply system in the automotive industry, and the interface structure between them, is illustrated in Figure 3.10.

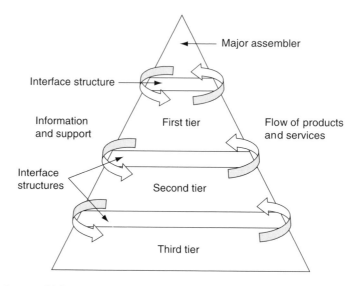

Fig. 3.10. *A pyramidal supply system*

Within this automotive industry example there are multiple layers or tiers roughly delineated by the size of the firms and their roles in the supply chain. At the apex of the pyramid sits the final assembler, who is supplied with subassemblies by first-tier suppliers. In turn, these first-tier companies are supplied by a larger number of second-tier suppliers. These second-tier suppliers have their own subcontractors who provide them with specialist process abilities. In some instances there may even be fourth- and fifth-tier suppliers. Within this tiering structure it is the responsibility of the customer tier to organise, communicate and nurture the level below. Thus, the assembler takes responsibility for the welfare of the first-tier suppliers, the first-tier that of the second-tier firms, and so on down the pyramid. In the context of social housing, the RSL could be at the apex of the pyramid, with cost and design consultants and main contractor as their first-tier suppliers. The second tier could comprise the specialist and trade subcontractors, with their material and component suppliers forming the third tier. A variation on this structure would be where the main contractor occupies the apex of the pyramid. This is similar to the structure adopted by Defence Estates in its prime contracting procurement approach.

A very advanced form of interface structure between a customer and a supplier is where organisational boundaries become blurred, as shown in Figure 3.11. The assignments of typical focus teams further illustrate that the parties are not only jointly handling the day-to-day operational business but are also holding joint board meetings and cooperating on strategic issues such as innovation, process integration and market research.

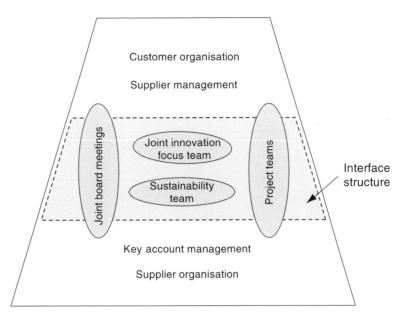

Fig. 3.11. An advanced interface structure between a customer and a supplier

An alternative to the pyramid is the cluster structure, which is illustrated in Figure 3.12. This is an idea developed in the Reading Construction Forum's report *Value for Money* and piloted by Defence Estates in the *Building Down Barriers* project. In this approach a prime contractor is appointed to work with key supply partners, known as cluster leaders, who set the general responsibility of designing and delivering a significant element of the building – the groundworks and substructure, the superstructure, the services, and so on.

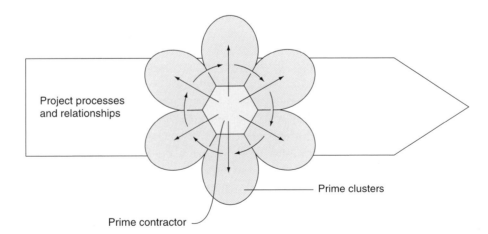

Fig. 3.12. Structuring of supply systems using clusters

This allows the prime contractor to improve in an integrated fashion the process for designing and delivering the overall building as well as the materials and the components that go into its main elements. It means the client has a single contractual relationship with the construction team. The contract is held by the prime contractor (usually a main contractor, although the role can be undertaken by other members of the construction team). The team is stable and consists of designers, the prime contractor and suppliers who have a long-term contract with the client for a series of projects. This means that the team's performance can be improved from project to project, and communication across the interface structures developed, as shown in Figure 3.13.

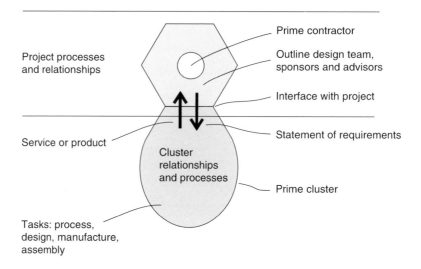

Fig. 3.13. *The interface between project processes and a supply cluster*

Within the context of longer-term relationships and structures, 'big picture mapping' techniques can be used to develop a clearer understanding of the key features of business and project processes. These maps can help in visualising the flows of information and physical objects within the main phases of development projects and the processes within each partner's business. They can be helpful in identifying the barriers to the integration of the resources at the interfaces between the organisations within their core processes. Such maps can also be used to identify waste and hence find an appropriate way to remove, or at least reduce, it. At this level of detail the maps are not intended to provide fine detail but rather to help identify the main intra- and interorganisational relationships and activities, and the individuals, teams and organisations involved. The use of such mapping techniques is also useful in creating buy-in to the process-oriented approach from the practitioners involved. An additional benefit is that the mapping of processes and relationships can be used to help anticipate the impact of possible change in one part of the process on another. While many of the organisations within the social housing sector already map their business processes these need to be integrated with those of their partners in order to form an overall 'big picture map'. The BPiPG used seven such maps: 'strategy setting', 'inception', 'business case', 'pre-contract', 'on site', 'post-completion' and 'supply chains'.

3.18. The key actions to be taken by RSLs

These are presented as an implementation audit table.

RSL implementation audit table

Actions	By when	Specific actions required	What implementation looks like
Promote the restructuring of supply chains and interface structures			

3.19. The key collective actions to be taken

Actions	By when	Specific actions required	What implementation looks like
Each partner to develop maps of 'who' does 'what', 'where', 'when', 'how' and 'why' within their organisations and how their people, organisational structure, information and physical flows and processes interface with those of their suppliers and customers			
Partners to collectively map processes and organisational structures to help identify 'who' does 'what', 'where', 'when', 'how' and 'why' at the interface between the organisations, in the main phases of the development process, and in the key supply chains in order to develop 'big picture maps'			
Partners to develop appropriate interface structures with their partners, including having in place the most appropriate people, information systems, procedures and organisational structures supported by the appropriate equipment, plant and learning			
Partners to use process mapping techniques to identify: ○ the main sources of influence, leverage, knowledge and resources within the relationship and processes; ○ the key areas for the removal of waste within and between the partners such as waiting, defects, overproduction, overlapping of roles and duplication, and contingency; ○ the opportunities to add value and increase mutual competitive advantage			
Change processes and procedures to improve integration and information and physical flows in order to reduce waste and add value			

3.20. The key barriers to be addressed

Key barriers	Proposed solutions
Providing the closer and longer-term relationships needed to encourage openness and transparency in relation to processes and to justify the considerable time and resources needed to map them effectively	
Providing the closer and longer-term relationships needed to support the investment of time and resources in continuously reshaping and improving processes and ensuring the appropriate amount of asset specificity	
The lack of appropriate mapping tools in construction generally and the social housing sector in particular	
The complexity, variability and uniqueness of the processes associated with scheme developments particularly upstream in the process in terms of regulatory and funding regimes	
The present lack of involvement of specialist and trade subcontractors downstream in the process and the other members of supply chains	
The present limited sharing of information and knowledge in much of the development process	

Element 5. Management of costs and risk and the provision of incentives

Traditionally most organisations involved in the construction process have viewed themselves as entities that exist independently from others. In this approach, organisations seek to achieve cost reductions, unload risk, or improve profit at the expense of the other participants. There is a growing realisation that this opportunistic behaviour, where costs and risks are simply transferred upstream or downstream in the process, does not make them, or the supply chain as a whole, any more competitive. Ultimately all costs will make their way to the marketplace, to be reflected in the price paid by the end user. Instead the BPiPG's model seeks to make the process as a whole more competitive through the value the partners add and the costs they reduce overall whilst increasing mutual competitive advantage. This approach recognises that in the more advanced forms of partnering real competition is no longer between RSLs and their suppliers but between one RSL and its supply chains and other RSLs and their suppliers.

There are a number of aspects to optimising value for all parties in the BPiPG's approach. The application of the Housing Corporation's HQIs and feedback from tenants and previous schemes is used to optimise the 'total value' (i.e. in terms of tenant satisfaction and value to RSLs including a reduction of whole-life costs and other important criteria) of the scheme for a given cost. Capital costs are managed during the development of the design on the basis of a target cost. This is driven by value analysis, value management and value engineering techniques. The experience of the BPiPG is showing that the greater openness and transparency associated with the more collaborative working in partnering allows the partners to undertake more meaningful value analysis, management and engineering. In addition, a combination of the more open relationships and more transparent processes can lead to the joint identification of risks and their associated costs that can either be 'designed out' or incorporated into a risk register where they are quantified and allocated to the partner most able to manage them. In the longer term this should result in greater certainty in out-turn costs for the RSL and profits for the contractor. It also ensures that risks and contingencies are only priced once within the process and are not used opportunistically by any of the participants. Financial incentives can also be used to further encourage collaboration, openness, creativity and innovation, and to help overcome resistance to innovation and cultural change.

In the BPiPG's approach, the agreement between the parties includes a guaranteed maximum price (GMP), contract sum, target cost (pre-contract) and target cost (post-contract) (see Figure 3.14). The target cost (pre-contract) allows the contractor to participate in the design process with a view to achieving an anticipated construction cost that is lower than the RSL's construction budget. The contract sum is the cost for the fully defined and detailed scope of the works as included for in the construction contract. The GMP is to limit the RSL's absolute financial liability under the construction contract, and is made up of the contract sum together with an evaluation of the work areas not fully defined, or risk items. The GMP is deemed to include the intention of the project to provide residential accommodation that complies with the objectives of the project at the time of the signing of the contract, and the attitudes and collaborative approach embodied in the partnering charter.

The target cost (post-contract) represents the partnership's target for cost

Fig. 3.14. *The BPiPG's approach to agreement*

reduction through continuous improvement. It is set by the mutual agreement of the partners and initially could, for example, be set at 10% below the contract sum. Should the final sum payable to the main contractor fall between the target cost and the GMP the main contractor is entitled to retain all the savings below the target cost. This can be viewed as a guaranteed minimum price. If the GMP is exceeded then the main contractor will bear all of the total extra cost unless the RSL increases the requirements of the project beyond those agreed when the contract was signed. If this eventuality should occur, the final impact of the change can be added to the GMP and contract sum together with a proportional increase to the target cost.

In order to achieve best value over the life of the project, both the capital and operational costs must be optimised. The key costs over the life of the scheme include:

○ capital cost;
○ acquisition cost;
○ maintenance and service cost;
○ repair costs;

○ training costs;
○ security and cleaning costs;
○ energy and utility costs;
○ decommissioning and disposal costs.

Optimising both the capital and operational costs is key, and consideration should be given to the following:

○ procuring housing that is functional, durable, maintainable, sustainable and efficient;
○ integration of both the design and construction of housing with future asset management;
○ assessing in detail future expenditure on the scheme;
○ assessing and managing future risks;
○ integration of the whole team, including asset or facilities management.

The key advantage of undertaking whole-life costing profiles for proposed developments is that both the capital and operational costs can be assessed against alternative designs and specifications at an early stage in the scheme development. Whole-life cost profiles provide a tool for evaluating alternative design and specification options to establish maintenance, repair and replacement strategies. However, there is a need for the development of better tools and more information on the durability of alternative materials and components, their energy and maintenance profiles, and sustainability. This means shifting the emphasis from the economic assessment of the capital costs of projects to using a whole-life approach is currently difficult. The problems include forecasting accuracy, lack of appropriate historical data, professional accountability, rapid changes in technology, social and fashion changes, changing legislation, capital versus operating budgets, and the underpinning theory of discounting.

In the case of the difficulties associated with forecasting accuracy, the BPiPG sees a possible solution in the use of risk analysis, whereby the uncertainty of future events can be evaluated against the robustness of assumptions to add confidence levels in final decisions. The BPiPG has also demonstrated the limitations of using historical data to predict future performance. Although each of the RSLs in the BPiPG have some useful sources of historical data about maintenance, energy usage, operating costs and life expectancies of materials, components and systems, it has proved difficult to create a comprehensive and robust database that can be used even by the four RSLs in the group. Even if the creation of such a comprehensive database existed now, the view of the BPiPG is that it would need to be used with great caution, since historical information is highly dependent upon the context in which it was collected. For example, the BPiPG has found that the operating costs of schemes differ due to the variable durability of materials, components and systems and the effects of their interaction with each other, the environment and, indeed, the users of the building. In addition, different occupancy profiles, locations, environmental factors, management policies, quality of the original construction, possible premature damage and inadequacies in the building process all affect the integrity of the data. A further complicating factor is that new technologies and methods and systems of construction are always being added. As a consequence, rather than focus on historical data, the BPiPG is estimating operating costs from first principles using context-specific databases for the routine comparison of predicted and actual performance. Elemental targets and individual work items can then act as benchmarks both for design and subsequent operation. Where cost overruns occur, the cost management process can focus on the reasons why and on implementing strategies that will ensure that overall cost limits on that scheme are not exceeded. This information can also be used as feedback for the design of future schemes. In this way, accountability in relation to whole-life costs becomes more about issues of methodology, capability and process.

A further complication in shifting the emphasis from capital costs to whole-life costs lies in the internal barriers that have been created by RSLs between capital and operating budgets. A whole-life approach relies fundamentally on the ability to spend more money initially in order to make overall savings, and if this cannot occur then the entire process becomes pointless. It is necessary, therefore, that RSLs remove these internal divisions and treat project budgets as inclusive of initial and recurrent cash flows.

The lack of experience and expertise of practitioners in relation to whole-life costs is a further difficulty. In the past, the RSLs' consultants and contractors were not accountable for the accuracy of their inputs in relation to whole-life costs since it can take many years to test whether their predictions are valid. Traditionally, the main contractors' responsibilities have been limited to the extent of the defects liability period. With the development of longer-term relationships associated with strategic partnering, consultants and main contractors will now be linked to individual schemes for at least the duration of a framework or term agreement. As this could be for a period of five or more years, this will no doubt concentrate the minds of consultants and contractors and their suppliers on the accuracy of their predictions in relation to whole-life performance. More importantly, it should, over time, provide an incentive and a framework for the development of more effective whole-life cost management methodologies, processes and tools. However, the early experience from Defence Estates and its prime contracting approach has identified that main contractors and their suppliers are presently reluctant to take on the additional burden of risk that this entails. The BPiPG discussed the possibility of main contractors taking on the responsibility for building elements that fail before the end of their predicted life but the contractors were reluctant to take on this additional responsibility, as it would radically change the nature of their businesses from contracting to longer-term investment companies.

Discounting is a further problem in whole-life costing. Discounting is generally regarded as a complex and controversial process as savings in cost are not completely recouped in the reduction in the private finance requirement, and therefore the long-term cashflows, of the RSL. The example below demonstrates the nature of the problem.

If a saving of £100 in capital cost resulted in an increase of £75 in the net present value (NPV) of whole-life costs, an overall improvement in the whole-life costs of £25 would result. However, if the grant rate was 68% (the headline rate for general needs housing), the saving of £100 would result in a reduction of grant of £68 in grant and £32 in loan debt. The RSL would have to pay back to the Housing Corporation £68 and incur a net loss to its cashflow of £43:

Whole-life gain

Reduction in capital cost	£100
Increase in lifecycle NPV	£75
NPV of net whole-life gain	£25

Reduction in the Housing Corporation social housing grant

Capital reduction of cost of works	£100
Reduction in eligible grant	£68
Net reduction in private finance	£32

Net gain/loss to RSL project cashflow

NPV of net whole-life gain	£25
Reduction in grant	£68
Net loss	£43

The example above shows the potential net effect of regulations controlling the eligibility of the social housing grant on value engineering of whole-life costings. In this case they create a disincentive for the RSL to reduce whole-life costs. The interrelationship between social housing grant regulations and value engineering require careful analysis and should be the subject of further research.

Because of the uncertainty over the life of building elements, different methodologies were discussed. One proposal was to weight the effect of the savings in the NPV of the lifecycle savings in order to reduce their impact on decision-making. For example, if a decrease in capital cost of £100 resulted in an increase in the NPV of £99, then the capital costs would be reduced and the net gain would be £1 to the RSL. However, because of the uncertainty of the accuracy of the assessment of the NPV of the reduced specification introduced as a result of the reduction in the capital costs, a weighting of 90% could be introduced in respect of capital savings. Thus, the decision to reduce the capital cost by £100 would only be made if the saving to the NPV were more than £110.

What is clear from the work of the BPiPG and others is that industry-agreed norms for the development of whole-life costing methodologies are now urgently required. Although the Building Research Establishment (BRE) and others have undertaken some work, there is not as yet a robust methodology for use in the social housing sector. It is also important that individual stakeholders from within RSLs and other bodies buy into the concept of whole-life costing as a legitimate methodology that requires developing, rather than dismissing it as an undeveloped methodology which does not sit well with Housing Corporation capital systems.

More collaborative relationships should provide the culture and environment within which a more open and rigorous identification of risk can take place. Improved communication between the partners and the sharing of knowledge and understanding of the whole process should allow them to adopt a more structured and analytical approach to the management of risk, which reduces bias and opportunistic behaviour, fosters objectivity, and prompts a considered and equitable approach to risk allocation within the partnership. The early and ongoing involvement of partners in an RSL's projects means that risk management activities can be more effective as they can be undertaken in the very early stages of scheme developments where there is maximum scope for control over the future shape, direction and cost of the project, and its associated risks.

The BPiPG recommends the use of risk registers to help identify and evaluate the risks, and, where possible, design risks out of the process. Where they cannot be designed out they need to be accounted for in the GMP. Examples of such risk items could include the breaking out of additional obstructions encountered in the ground, late release of information to the contractor for construction, and consultant errors within the contract documentation. Other items of risk can be for elements not yet fully designed such as landscaping and works by statutory undertakers. The risk allowance to cover the estimated consequences of the occurrence of the risk and the division of responsibility between the partners' evaluation is agreed between all the parties, and the total risk allowance is added to the contract sum to give the GMP. In this way the GMP is developed to include identified risk areas in the project. The risk registers are monitored and updated throughout the design and construction periods, and any additional risks arising are added and any risks that have not occurred are removed. A typical risk register is shown below.

Risk	Risk allowance to cover estimated consequences of the occurrence of the risk	Responsibility for the risk (in percentage terms) between:		
		Client	Contractor	Consultant
Physical/material				
Consequential				
Social				
Political				
Financial				
Technical				

This percentage split can only be determined as the division of a series of risks between the project team members. In order to have more scope to balance risk, the project team should break risks down as finely as they can and examine the scope for capping risk. For example, one project team member might take a risk on up to a value of £40,000 and for costs arising from the same risk. Beyond £40,000 another member of the team might take it on.

A number of incentives can also be introduced by RSLs with the objectives of encouraging collaborative behaviour, teamworking, changes in attitudes, continuous improvement and the adding and sharing of value. A major incentive for consultants and contractors is the prospect of repeat work. There are also a number of financial incentives. These can include the appropriate sharing of the difference between the GMP and the budget for the project between the RSL and contractor. And also the sharing of the differences between the contract sum and the GMP. In order to provide further incentive to keep the total cost down, the partners may also set the target cost at, say, 10% below the contract sum. Any difference between the target cost and the GMP can then be shared between the RSL and the contractor. A further incentive is that if the total out-turn cost at final account should fall below the target cost then the contractor retains the amount below the target cost. Incentives should also be extended to specialist and trade subcontractors and material suppliers in recognition of the major contribution they can make to adding value and reducing costs. If they propose a change in the product or process that leads to savings, these can be shared and apportioned on an agreed percentage as in the following example:

RSL	50%
Contractor/developer	25%
Specialist or trade subcontractor or supplier	25%

3.21. The key actions to be taken by RSLs

These are presented as an implementation audit table.

RSL implementation audit table

Actions	By when	Specific actions required	What implementation looks like
Strike the right balance between quality and cost			
Be open with your partners in relation to the finances and budget for individual schemes			
Insist that target costing is used to manage costs during design			
Be prepared to provide financial incentives to encourage and support more collaborative behaviour and reward continuous improvement against measurable targets such as HQIs			
Avoid overly prescriptive designs and specifications and gradually make the shift to providing your suppliers with performance specifications rather than solutions			
Ensure appropriate fees for your consultants and that your main contractor's margins are ring fenced			
Buy into and encourage whole-life costing and share your knowledge of the whole-life performance of your schemes with your partners			
Use your longer-term relationships with your suppliers to progressively extend the period of time for which they are responsible for the performance of your schemes			
Collect data on the accuracy of the projections by your supply chain on the whole-life performance and costs of their designs and specifications for your schemes			
Insist on the use of risk registers for scheme developments			

3.22. The key actions to be taken by consultants

Actions	By when	Specific actions required	What implementation looks like
Ensure that the main contractor's margins are ring fenced			
Adopt target costing to manage costs during the design			
See design as the key to cost and risk reduction, with both being managed out as much as possible before they occur			
Ensure that all the partners to have access to the updated cost plan during the design process			
Help the partners to use value analysis to define what value is attached to different aspects of the design and performance specification			
Encourage the partners to use value management and engineering to reduce costs and add value			
Support the partners in working together openly and collaboratively to identify, define, measure and share risks appropriately according to the ability of the partners to manage them			
Help the partners to use communication and improvement tools such as value management and brainstorming			
Help the partners to complete a risk register in a way that avoids opportunistic behaviour. Constantly keep the register up to date as the scheme develops			

3.23. The key barriers to be addressed

Key barriers	Proposed solutions
Ensuring the involvement of cross-organisational and functional teams in managing costs	
Ensuring cost reduction focuses on waste and inefficiency rather than on reducing functionality, performance, quality and profit margins	
Present lack of involvement of specialist and trade subcontractors and suppliers in design and cost planning and value management	
Combating the tendency to overemphasise, cutting costs at the expense of adding value	
Lack of robust cost data	
Lack of focus on whole-life costs	
Lack of data and methodologies for the determination of whole-life costs	
Funding regimes which differentiate between capital and whole-life costs	

Element 6. Monitoring the relationship: demonstrating added value and mutual advantage

The closer relationships between the main parties involved in partnering, and, in the case of strategic partnering the longer-term relationships, increases the need to monitor the effectiveness of the relationships. In the context of social housing, careful monitoring is needed to:

○ reinforce top-down commitment to the new relationships;
○ encourage the bottom-up involvement of individuals and groups;
○ identify opportunities for further improvement;
○ ensure openness and transparency in the relationships;
○ measure performance to demonstrate continuous improvement leading to increased value for money and mutual competitive advantage;
○ constantly review the overall effectiveness of the partnering approach.

Monitoring refers to all procedures employed to evaluate whether the relationship meets the objectives agreed upon when setting up the partnership. Monitoring processes should be based on improvement targets in relation to the HQIs and KPIs as well as those set for the development of the relationship. In this way, feedback is not only obtained on 'what has been achieved' but also on 'how it was accomplished'.

Monitoring project performance and the development of the relationship

The performance of the Clarence Hotel project was benchmarked against a number of metrics including:

○ *Client satisfaction – service*. Scored out of 10 at monthly site meetings.
○ *Predictability – cost*. Each month, during the construction process, financial statements were produced with the change in cost reflected as a percentage of the contract sum.
○ *Predictability – time*. Progress was monitored against the programme on a monthly basis.
○ *Defects*. The following were monitored: overall defects, breakdown of defects by response time, overall defect completions within the timescale, and defects logged and completed per month.
○ *Safety*. An independent safety consultant visited the site each month and provided a report including a score for safety performance. These were available at the monthly site meetings.
○ *Supply chain management*. The performance of suppliers was regularly monitored and scored, with scores being fed back to suppliers, highlighting good practice and identifying areas for improvement.
○ *Client performance*. There were nine metrics relating to Devon and Cornwall Housing Association's performance as a client. These were:
  – standard of the brief;
  – understanding of, and commitment to, partnering;
  – flexibility of approach;
  – commitment to whole-life costing;
  – involvement of other departments;
  – lines of communication;
  – receptiveness to innovation;
  – feedback on defects;
  – relationships with other partners.

Their performance against these 'relationship' metrics was measured on a three-monthly basis.

As public money is involved in the social housing sector, developments are governed by regulations that require transparency, and the Housing Corporation and RSLs are subject to high levels of scrutiny. HM Treasury's *Government Construction Procurement Guidance*, Guidance Note No. 4, requires that good, clear records be maintained to demonstrate that parties have worked together to reach decisions, and how best value has accrued and probity and propriety have been maintained. Proper accountability must be demonstrated. The National Audit Office also requires that expenditure is properly accounted for and that value for money is being obtained. As partnering is essentially about greater openness and transparency, then there should be no real conflict between the more advanced forms of partnering and the transparency needed for auditing purposes. Indeed, in such an approach the parties should be able to provide more evidence about the nature of relationships and performance improvements than is possible in more traditional, and more closed, price-competitive approaches to procurement. The main danger, however, is that relationships can become too cosy so that best value is not being achieved. The ECI publication *Partnering in the Social Housing Sector* outlines the importance of establishing an audit trail and suggests sources of audit information for scheme developments. The BPiPG would also recommend that as a further safeguard the internal auditors are kept appraised of the development of the partnering approach, and that they are provided with the flow of audit information agreed in the policy and strategy element of the model.

The information from the monitoring of the relationship can be fed back into the continuous improvement process. Continuous improvement implies the continual and methodical measurement of performance against a set of appropriate metrics and then seeking better ways of doing things. In order for continuous improvement to work it is vital that a systematic methodology is in place whereby data are collected, analysed and reviewed in an ongoing process (e.g. on a monthly basis) by the project team and the partnering organisations.

Monitoring continuous improvement

The Fortfield Road project has metrics based on issues for which the consultants and main contractors are responsible. Minutes are kept to ensure that issues arising have been addressed and closed out in a timely and consistent manner. Guinness provides feedback, including a score out of 10, on these indicators on a regular basis throughout the progress of the scheme, including design and site meetings. If there is no particular satisfaction or dissatisfaction the score for the month is 5. These measurements of performance are analysed in order to provide early warning of problems and to identify where opportunities have been taken to improve performance and add value.

Each of the monthly scores will be used to provide a mean score at practical completion and at the end of the defects liability period. The scores are plotted on performance radar diagrams, and trends identified and acted upon.

The process of improvement needs to take place over a considerable period of time, which means only a small part of its potential can be realised within the length and closeness of relationships and the degree of commitment and allocation of supplier assets associated with project-specific partnering. This means that to be fully effective, continuous improvement needs to be applied within the context of long-term relationships between the client, consultants and the main contractor. It also indicates a need for close and long-term relationships between the main contractor and specialist and trade subcontractors and suppliers. Evidence from other sectors also suggests that RSLs will need to impose considerable pressure on its partners if improvements in the supply chains are to be made and sustained, and complacency and loss of competitiveness avoided. Figure 3.15 proposes eight forces that can be applied to drive continuous improvement in the supply chain.

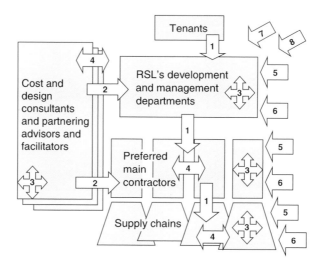

Key
1 The tenants' changing needs, tastes and aspirations
2 Support, facilitation, advice and performance measurement
3 Intraorganisational improvement activities
4 Interfirm competitive rivalry and creative tension
5 New entrants to the supply chain
6 Substitutes
7 Continuity of funding and flow of schemes
8 support by national and local government and their agencies

Fig. 3.15. Applying forces for improvement in the supply chains

The evidence from other industries also shows that main contractors need to impose similar pressure on their specialist and trade subcontractors and suppliers of material and components. However, given the size of many subcontractors and the resources available to them, they will need the help of main contractors in raising their performance. This can, for example, take the form of joint investment in training and by providing them with expert support and advice in key aspects of their business. This is known as supplier development.

Midas Homes assess the performance of their suppliers of materials using the following criteria:

- O technical support;
- O sales/order office response;
- O delivery adherence, quantities, driver cooperation;
- O quality of materials;
- O waste management/packaging;
- O problem-solving.

Each criterion is scored out of 10, giving a total possible score of 60.

3.24. The key actions to be taken by RSLs

These are presented as an implementation audit table.

RSL implementation audit table

Actions	By when	Specific actions required	What implementation looks like
Demonstrate top-down/upstream commitment to monitoring performance by regularly measuring your own performance Ensure that the new relationships and processes are regularly monitored against clear performance metrics and targets for improvement Ensure that the eight forces in Figure 3.15 are being applied to continuously improve performance and to combat complacency and the rationalisation of failure			

3.25. The key actions to be taken by main contractors

Actions	By when	Specific actions required	What implementation looks like
Monitor the performance of RSLs, consultants and other participants upstream in the process Monitor your own performance and that of your key specialist and trade subcontractors and suppliers downstream in the process Support and help your specialist and trade subcontractors in using quality and productivity improvement tools and techniques such as statistical process control and CALIBRE (a site productivity measurement tool) Encourage your specialist and trade subcontractors to empower their operatives and involve and train them in performance measurement and continuous improvement			

3.26. The key collective actions to be taken

Actions	By when	Specific actions required	What implementation looks like
Exploit the longer-term partnering relationships to embrace the philosophy of continuous improvement and total quality management			
Use a structured approach, such as Business Excellence, to measure and improve partners' enablers and results, inputs and outputs, processes, and their relationships with the other partners			
Identify, classify and collect the information and data needed to evaluate current development performance and to monitor the effectiveness of the emerging partnership			
Use HQIs to add value for the end user			
Regularly measure your performance and business results against a range of appropriate and mutually agreed KPIs			
Accumulate and present the evidence to demonstrate that, year by year and project by project, you are continuously reducing waste, adding value and increasing mutual competitive advantage			
Produce improvement curves, radar diagrams and other methods of demonstrating the impact of your continuous improvement activities			
Seek out and react to feedback from tenants, the RSL's housing managers and operating departments, and other key stakeholders			
Give continuous 360° evaluation and feedback on performance			
Benchmark the performance of your supply chain against other supply chains in the social housing sector and the rest of construction, and, in the longer term, other sectors of the economy			
From time to time, use means, such as external consultants, to verify the quality and operation of your arrangements and to determine that your relationship is continuously adding value and increasing mutual competitive advantage			

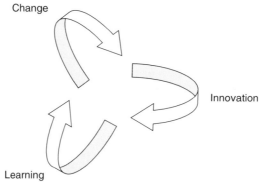

Fig. 3.16. The relationship between change, innovation and learning

3.27. The key barriers to be addressed

Key barriers	Proposed solutions
The present barriers to openness and rigourous monitoring of performance presented by the short-term and adversarial relationships and opportunistic behaviour throughout much of construction's supply systems	
The current limited involvement of specialist and trade subcontractors and suppliers in monitoring and improving performance	
Providing sufficient influence and leverage to justify the constant and open monitoring of performance of the supply chain	
The allocation of sufficient time and resources for monitoring the effectiveness of the new relationships	
The lack of quality culture and problem-solving skills throughout the supply chain but particularly downstream of the main contractor in the process	
The main contractor's lack of expertise in developing suppliers coupled with limited time and resources for supplier development downstream in the process	
The change- and risk-averse culture of construction and the reluctance to adopt new technologies and working methods	

Element 7. Changing the culture and developing people

Implementing the BPiPG's holistic approach to partnering in an environment of continuous improvement is a challenging and complex innovation that requires considerable learning. The relationship between change, innovation and learning is shown in Figure 3.16. This illustrates the need for innovation supported by learning if organisations are to cope with increasing pressure for change in their business environment. It also suggests that if the learning is to be effective in maintaining competitive advantage then the rate of learning must be equal to or greater than the rate of change in the external environment.

The difference between learning and training

It is important to differentiate between training and learning. Training involves people having solutions presented to them, whereas learning involves people doing something for themselves.

Today, organisations have to cope with increasing pressures such as rapid changes in technology, the rise of e-commerce, situations where customers and suppliers can be both competitors and allies, and a change in emphasis from quantity to quality and from products to services. The explosion of knowledge and ever-faster means of communication are also radically altering today's business environment, and anticipating changes in the market is becoming more problematic. In addition, customers are demanding bundles of increasingly smarter products and services.

Clearly, the pace of change is accelerating as never before, and organisations need to chart their way through an increasingly complex environment.

New ways of addressing this increasing complexity are emerging, including the growing awareness of the value of the specialised knowledge embedded within organisations in their people, processes and routines. There is a growing awareness of the role of this knowledge in supporting innovation to respond to these changes in the wider business environment. More and more organisations are recognising the importance of acquiring and utilising increasing amounts of knowledge if they are to make the changes necessary to remain competitive and provide best value. This means that today a firm's competitive advantage increasingly depends more than anything on its knowledge – or more specifically on:

○ what it knows;
○ how fast it can know something new (learning);
○ how effectively it uses what it knows and translates it into effective innovative action.

Partnering is also providing a means to work and learn more effectively within and between organisations, as the knowledge developed from learning can be shared more easily and effectively with the members of the partnership. Knowledge management is the term often used to describe the management routines and techniques that can help people in organisations share what they know. This is increasingly being seen as a way to enable organisations to exploit the knowledge and learning of their own people to add value and increase competitive advantage throughout their supply chains.

Different types of knowledge

It is important to recognise that there are different types of knowledge. Knowledge that is systematic and easily codified and communicated is called *explicit knowledge*. Books and Codes of Practice are examples of this kind of knowledge.

Tacit knowledge is more akin to wisdom. Although understood it is rarely described and more difficult to disseminate. This form of knowledge normally resides in peoples' heads; for example, 'know-how' rather than of 'know-what'.

It is becoming increasingly apparent that both forms of knowledge are very important and both need feed into each other in what has been called a 'spiral of knowledge'. Tacit knowledge can be converted into explicit knowledge by articulation, and explicit knowledge can be used to develop an individual's cognitive understanding by a process of internalisation.

Knowledge is not simply data or information. Information is what data become when we summarise and interpret it. Having knowledge about something involves the ability to understand, judge and interpret rather than just being told about it. Knowledge is accumulated both through experience and education.

The conversion of data and information into know-how can increase organisational effectiveness and enhance business outcomes, including greater shareholder value, repeat business for satisfied clients and knowledge and know-how growth. However, this is dependent on:

Knowledge development (supply)
For example:

○ project and business experience;
○ workshops, seminars, training courses and on-line training;

Different types of knowledge (contd)

O   internal briefings;
O   peer reviews and mentoring;
O   work shadowing within and outside the organisation;
O   project evaluation and debriefing;
O   applying the knowledge–information–knowledge cycle.

Knowledge exploitation
For example:

O   application of know-how (knowledge exploitation);
O   business management best practice;
O   project teamwork – synergy, the whole is greater than the parts;
O   client relationships;
O   virtual business units;
O   skill groups – local and global;
O   5-year strategy and new business development.

In the past it has been found to be very difficult, if not impossible, to apply knowledge management within projects as it is difficult to transfer knowledge from project to project when project teams are assembled in an *ad hoc* way. Knowledge transfer from project to business, business to project, and from business to business is also problematic given the contractual nature of most traditional business relationships in construction and the culture of blame they generate. However, with the emergence of longer-term relationships through strategic partnering and supply chain management such barriers can gradually be removed to allow more and more sharing of knowledge between businesses and project teams and between businesses. However, it must be recognised that even in longer-term business relationships in stable supply chains there are still considerable barriers to the transfer of knowledge and understanding.

There are two main dimensions to learning and knowledge acquisition – technical and social. Much of the guidance most readily available to construction is still strongly influenced by the technical aspects. *Introduction to Knowledge Management*, published by Construction Best Practice, suggests that knowledge management can be organised in five stages:

O   *Search*: seek out explicit and tacit knowledge internally and externally.
O   *Capture*: record the principles and core thinking of ideas and new knowledge.
O   *Articulate*: make the tacit knowledge explicit and communicate all knowledge throughout the organisation by means of presentations, meetings, working papers or reports.
O   *Apply*: harness the knowledge to address business problems, in particular by using project management tools and resources.
O   *Learn*: reflect on the process, review the experience and assess which parts of the process could be better managed.

In practice, the process of knowledge creation moves forward and backward through these stages in an iterative rather than cyclical way. Activity should be going on in all of these stages at any one time.

The experience of the BPiPG suggests that partnering requires elements of the social dimension of knowledge management. Partnering requires the partners to learn new personal and interorganisational skills. A partnership also provides an environment that is more supportive to aspects of the social dimension of knowledge management. There are three key aspects to the social perspective on learning: learning and knowledge acquisition is *socially constructed* as a *political process*, and it is shaped by the *organisational culture*. The idea of learning as a social construction can be seen as addressing some of the limitations of the technical approach, by acknowledging that information has little significance in its own right until people determine what the information means and agree to share it. The proponents of this approach argue that learning emerges from social interactions, normally in the work setting. The social perspective on organisational learning focuses on the way people make collective sense of their experiences at work. These experiences may derive from explicit sources such as financial information, or they may derive from tacit sources such as the intuition of skilled managers and consultants.

Partnering requires organisations to change their culture by reshaping the beliefs, values, and the attitudes and behaviour of the people involved. The extent of this culture change will be determined by the scope of the partnering approach to be adopted and the receptiveness and the degree of preparedness of the individuals and organisations involved. The more advanced forms of partnering will require considerable commitment to individual, organisational and interorganisational change and learning. The most necessary, and yet the most difficult changes to make, are those relating to intra- and interorganisational attitudes and behaviour.

The experience of the BPiPG suggests that as the partners work more closely together so both the need for learning, and the opportunities to learn increase. Individual and collective learning within individual organisations can be extended to interorganisational learning. In this way, partnering can extend the scope of learning from beyond the boundary of the organisation or project to the boundary formed by all the organisations within the partnering arrangement. The more open and trusting relationships also allow knowledge to be passed more freely between organisations. Successfully transferring embedded forms of knowledge between organisations is more likely to be effective in longer-term relationships associated with strategic partnering, as these are more likely to promote the emergence of a culture of sharing, openness and trust. Indeed, this sharing of learning can help in understanding the many different and overlapping cultures that exist within the participating organisations, and the work of the BPiPG suggests that much of the early learning associated with partnering needs to focus on understanding each other's corporate cultures, objectives, aspirations and ways of working. Learning in cross-organisational teams forces people to confront multiple viewpoints and perspectives that they might otherwise ignore. The BPiPG has also found that simply transferring knowledge between the partners is insufficient for innovation to occur, as organisations need to be able to recognise the value of the knowledge, understand it and apply it appropriately if it is to be used to good effect. However, the challenges of learning in such cross-organisational teams should not be underestimated as they are even greater than those identified for individual learning or organisational learning. Needs and values must be identified and negotiated, conflicts addressed and different ideas brought together. It also needs to be

Organisational learning

Proponents of the *social perspective* on organisational learning argue that it involves making joint sense of data and the observation and emulation of skilled practitioners and its socialisation into community practice. A central idea is that much crucial organisational knowledge exists not on paper, nor in the heads of individuals but in the community as a whole. Hence, learning takes place either through expansion of the community to incorporate new individuals, or through the adoption of new forms of more collaborative behaviour and practices.

The idea of organisational learning as a *political process* recognises that organisational defensive routines impede the sharing of learning and knowledge because people often feel the need to protect themselves from political threat. If knowledge is socially constructed by individuals and groups, it is inevitable that particular interpretations will suit the interests of some and harm the interests of others. This means that the interpretation of information will be directly influenced by power relations. Departments, functional groups and project teams will organise consciously to present information internally and externally in a way that suits their purpose. Indeed, it could be argued that it is a necessary responsibility of departmental managers to ensure that the people they represent, including their roles and outputs, are presented, or spun, positively to external stakeholders – whether these are senior managers, shareholders, the media or public auditors. Therefore, open and honest dialogue is needed amongst different occupational cultures, departments and in the organisation as a whole. Although the idea of learning as a political process is touched upon by many proponents of the technical school, it is from the perspective that it is a persistent problem that needs to be overcome and nullified if learning is to take place. From the social perspective, however, the goal of eliminating organisational politics is seen as naïve and idealistic – because politics is a natural feature of any social process and will not somehow go away, and approaches to organisational learning must thus embrace political processes within them.

The third significant contribution from the social perspective is the notion of learning as a *cultural artefact*. Learning is something that takes place not just within the minds of individuals but in the interactions between people. It is discernible within the ways that people behave when working with others. Such patterns of behaviour are built up in the organisation through a process of socialisation. There has been some work linking learning processes to cultural traits. For example, a study has demonstrated that senior Japanese managers in a sample of more than 300 companies provided strong support for innovation, risk-taking, wide dissemination of information and broad involvement in decision-taking. This, alongside other studies, suggests that different national business cultures and traditions may lead to different learning processes, and perhaps also that the product or outcomes of learning may be different in one culture compared to another.

recognised that interorganisational relationships in construction have been adversarial for decades, which means that cross-organisational learning presents particular challenges.

Learning in partnering teams can be promoted through a number of mechanisms:

○ Clear and systematic commitment from top management within the partnering organisations and from upstream in the supply chain.

○ Identifying individual and collective learning needs and providing appropriate change and learning programmes.

○ The facilitation of the learning process within organisations and at the interface between the partners.

○ The learning of new skills and ways of working, which in turn supports further innovation.

○ Incentives and rewards for effective individual and collective learning.

○ Effective change systems, procedures and personnel policies – especially those concerned with incentives, rewards and appraisal.

○ Leaders, champions, coaches, steering groups or task forces to identify the need for individual and collective learning and to encourage and support them.

○ The allocation of time and resources to support learning to match the internal preparedness of the partners to the partnering approach.

○ Effective communication and diffusion of the new values through seminars, workshops, briefing groups, house journals, etc.

○ Reorganising the workforce to ensure that those employees and managers displaying the required traits occupy positions of influence.

○ Changing recruitment, selection and redundancy policies to alter the composition of the workforce so that promotion and employment prospects are dependent on those concerned possessing or displaying the beliefs and values the organisations in the partnership wish to adopt.

At the beginning of the implementation process the learning undertaken by the partners will need to focus on understanding the concept of partnering and the development of the new competencies, skills and expertise needed to make it work. This learning agenda will need to address the changes associated with each of the elements of the model – leadership, building new relationships, integrating processes, management of risk and value, and performance measurement. This learning needs to be individual and collective as well as both informal and formal.

Ways to learn

There are a number of opportunities for formal and collective learning about partnering, including:

○ attending courses, seminars and other public events;

○ organising in-house seminars, workshops and training courses;

○ joining organisations promoting change and learning such as 'Inside Industry UK – Construction' and the Construction Best Practice Clubs;

○ action learning;

○ learning from partnering advisors and facilitators;

○ inclusion of articles and case studies in staff magazines;

○ sharing of learning within project meetings;

○ away days.

There are also less formal and more individual ways of learning including:

○ purchase and reading of reports and good practice guides;

○ providing access to the internet and key websites such as 'Rethinking Construction' and the Housing Forum;

○ exchange of learning between individuals and organisations during normal working within scheme development projects.

As the model focuses on an RSL-led approach to partnering, the first learning needs to take place within RSLs as they raise the awareness of their own staff of the need for change and the nature of partnering, its benefits and concerns, and the barriers to its successful implementation.

Guinness Trust Housing Association runs in-house conferences four times a year. These range between one and four days' duration. These focus on 'rethinking construction' as well as on other issues. The events are used to keep development and maintenance staff from around the country informed about progress on new initiatives. They also provide an opportunity for consultation and the sharing of learning. Both in-house staff and external experts facilitate these events.

This early learning will need to focus on their pivotal role in introducing the new relationships, and will include policy and strategy development, supply chain leadership, supplier selection, and performance measurement. Later in its implementation, learning will need to be shared between the partners. Here the emphasis switches to identifying common issues and problems, developing joint commitment to the partnering approach, the exchange of information and knowledge, confronting barriers and addressing the tensions arising from different value systems.

A learning action plan

At the adoption stage of the partnering approach the partners need to begin identifying the skills needed and the subsequent learning programme, which should be shown in a learning action plan.

The progress towards partnering to add value and increase mutual advantage depends on building closer and more collaborative relationships between individuals at all levels within the participating organisations. Building robust, closer and more collaborative interorganisational relationships is difficult and requires the commitment of the people involved, and that they have the appropriate understanding of partnering and the required attitudes and behaviours. This means breaking with much of what might have been seen as being important in relationships in the past and changing intra- and interorganisational cultures. As an organisation's culture is locked into the beliefs, values and norms of each individual employee, and because these are so difficult to alter, organic change is likely to be slow unless there are substantial forces for change within the participating organisations or in the external environment. If substantial cultural changes are to be effected, then the key people at the interface between the partnering organisations must perceive tangible evidence of a supportive, trusting and committed relationship between the organisation and themselves. However, gaining such commitment is generally a more difficult and complex task than first envisaged. Although an increasing number of organisations engaged in social housing projects rationally accept the benefits of more collaborative approaches, their cultures are not readily compatible, and implementation often faces strong resistance to change.

The experience of the BPiPG suggests that facilitation is needed in implementing partnering and developing more collaborative relationships. Facilitators can play an important role in working with individuals and groups within the partnering organisations to help them prepare for partnering. They are also needed at the interface between the partnering organisations to help build close and collaborative relationships, confront the problems, form interface structures, promote and support collective learning, and integrate processes. Such facilitators need to have a deep understanding of the concept of partnering and the nature of intra- and interorganisational behaviour. They need to be able to work with the groups of people to help them understand and customise the new ways of working associated with partnering without having managerial responsibility for the groups involved. This separation of the responsibility for introducing the partnering approach and the responsibility for making it work can be helpful in developing the necessary openness and gaining the acceptance of all those involved. However, it is currently difficult to obtain the services of a facilitator with the necessary mix of knowledge, understanding and skills.

The role of the partnering advisor or facilitator

A facilitator is in many ways the link between good intentions and actions, and can provide a useful addition to some teams, particularly where the concept of teamwork and collaboration is relatively new. A facilitator needs to be particularly skilled in problem-solving, team dynamics and liaison.

The facilitator role is also valuable in educating the participants in the tools and techniques of partnering and continuous improvement – such as brainstorming, fishbone diagrams and Pareto diagrams.

A facilitator should be chosen carefully using the following criteria:

O   knowledge of, and enthusiasm for, partnering and continuous improvement;
O   capable of thinking broadly and seeing the bigger picture;
O   respect by peer group and senior management;
O   ability to withstand the stress and the frustration often associated with the change process;
O   skills to teach, coach, persuade and inform;
O   communication skills with clarity of speech and ideas;
O   sensitivity to interpersonal and interorganisational relationships and processes;
O   understanding of the context and culture of social housing.

Having started the process of relationship building, the cross-organisational teams need then to acquire skills in the use of the tools and techniques associated with continuous improvement, including:

O   input–output analysis;
O   process flow charts;
O   data collection;
O   scatter diagrams;
O   teamworking;
O   brainstorming;
O   problem identification and cause–effect diagrams;

○ Pareto diagrams*;
○ why–why analysis;
○ statistical tools.

They also need to learn how to map their business and project processes in order to identify:

○ all the steps in developing the scheme;
○ the information and physical flows;
○ the value stream;
○ what does and does not create value for the end user;
○ the critical success factors;
○ the barriers to improvement such as standing orders and administrative procedures.

These tools can then be applied using the plan–do–check–act cycle associated with continuous improvement within the new no-blame culture, where mistakes are seen as opportunities for improvement. Growing familiarity with these tools will allow the partners to generate ideas for driving out waste and adding value.

There are different types of learning, which reflect the degree of certainty and change in which the partners are operating. If partnering is to be effective the rate of learning undertaken by the partners must be equal to, or even greater than the rate of change in the external environment and in the development of the relationship. As can be seen from Figure 13.17, the most basic and least demanding form of learning is often referred to as 'single-loop learning'.

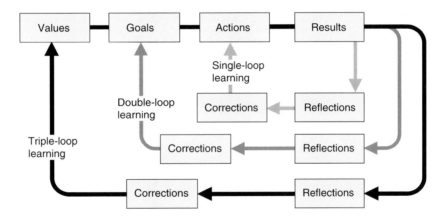

***Fig. 3.17.** The types of learning*

'Single-loop learning' is associated with training, and is most appropriate in a time of relative predictability and certainty. It consists simply of accumulating knowledge and skills and adapting behaviour towards the attainment of existing goals. The organisation reacts by correcting errors within the norms and values that

---

* In any improvement process, it is worthwhile distinguishing what is important and what is less so. The purpose of Pareto analysis is to distinguish between the 'vital few issues' and the 'trivial many'. It is a relatively straightforward technique that involves arranging items of information on the types of problem or causes of problems into their order of importance. This can be used to highlight areas where further decision-making will be useful.

form the organisation's well-established rationale. The existing norms are not questioned, and they remain directed towards the existing purpose of the organisation. Organisations in the social housing sector have become proficient at 'single-loop learning', developing an ability to scan the environment, set objectives and monitor the general performance of the system in relation to these objectives. This basic skill is often institutionalised in the form of information systems and standing orders designed to keep the organisation 'on course'. For example, budgets, employer's requirements and management controls often maintain single-loop learning by monitoring compliance with Housing Corporation SDS requirements, expenditures, turnover, profits, and other indications of performance to ensure that organisational activities remain within established limits.

Dismantling barriers to shared learning

'Employer's requirements' are usually substantial documents that have been built up over many years and modified to iron out errors and defects but now heavily restrict empowerment and innovation in the supply chains to scheme developments.

As well as models of the types of learning and knowledge acquisition, there are also models to help understand the *transfer* of knowledge. Many of these recognise that translating experience into knowledge and sharing it is not something that happens automatically. In fact, it takes a considerable amount of intent to create knowledge out of an experience and pass it on to other people within the same organisation. It is even more difficult to share that knowledge with other people within other organisations – even if they are in a close and collaborative interorganisational relationship. This involves a willingness to collectively reflect back on actions and outcomes before moving forward. In an organisation or a project team with a bias for action, the time for reflection may be hard to come by. Also, when it is a team rather than an individual that has produced the outcome, the task of translating experience into knowledge is compounded, because all the team members have to come to some understanding of *what* really happened and *why*. Many organisations allot no time to debriefing a project team or reviewing a just-completed task. This means that a team may have achieved an extraordinary success but the organisation may find itself unable to repeat the success because the team has not taken the time to build the knowledge about why it worked so well. The team had the experience but failed to capture the knowledge.

Figure 3.18 shows the steps that a team must take to translate experience from undertaking tasks into knowledge.

This is has been referred to as serial transfer. The third step in the process – the team explores the relationship between action and outcome – is seen as the most important in translating experience into knowledge. This arises out of the time and effort taken to make the connections between what the team did (actions) and what the outcome was. If it is to repeat the task in a few days or months it will need to introduce a further step, which is to modify its actions the next time, based on knowledge it has developed. This model can be seen as appropriate for project teams engaged in serial contracting as a result of longer-term relationships arising from partnering. As has been seen earlier in this report, the results in certain parts of

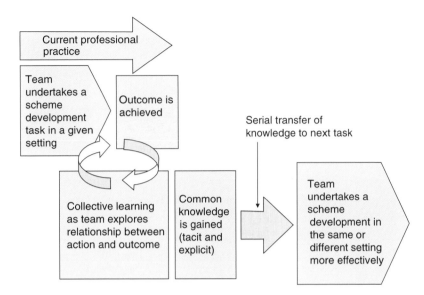

Fig. 3.18. *Transferring knowledge from project to project*

construction can be staggering, with up to 30% reduction in costs and 50% reduction in time.

For this approach to work effectively there must be a disciplined strategy that is carried out by active team members who are intent not only on achieving effective results but also on knowing how the results were achieved. Without such a clear strategy of continuous improvement and effective relationships between the members of the team it will not be clear what results were actually achieved and why, and any meaningful knowledge will not be captured.

The next model, shown in Figure 3.19, is needed to transfer knowledge across time and space, such as from one project team to another or from one development scheme to another. Although this is seen as being very challenging, again the results can be significant. Ford claims that they saved US $34 million in just one year by transferring ideas between vehicle operations plants. This model begins with the creation of knowledge – otherwise there would be nothing to transfer. Further additional steps are:

○ Find a method or system for transferring the knowledge to another group (or individual) that can reuse it. This will be largely determined by who the intended receiver is, the nature of the task, and the type of knowledge being transferred. Generally, the more explicit the knowledge the easier it is transferred.
○ Translate what has been learned into a form that others can use.
○ The receiving team or individuals adapts the knowledge for use in particular context.
○ The process repeats itself with the receiving team taking action on a new task.

The receiving team's action, having been adapted rather than simply adopted, may itself constitute an innovation.

These models provide some useful insights into the nature of learning, the acquisition of knowledge and its transfer, including:

○ there are different levels of learning for different situations;
○ there is no end to learning but only another turn of the cycle;

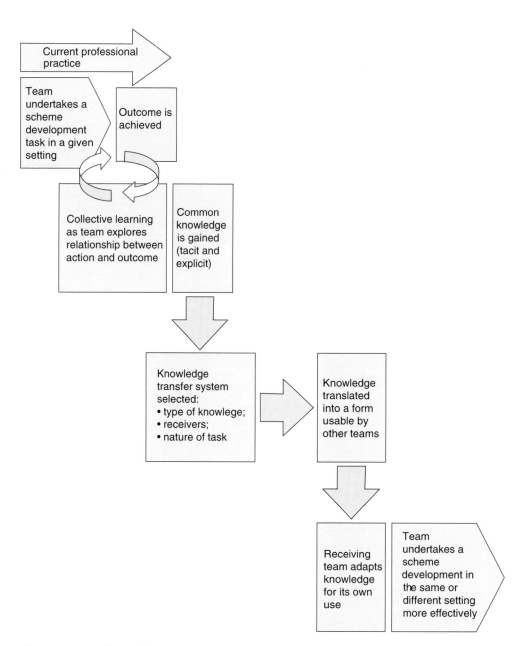

Fig. 3.19. *Transferring knowledge between project teams*

- ○ it involves taking action on real issues – termed action learning;
- ○ learners are not passive recipients but need to actively explore new concepts/ideas and test them in their environment;
- ○ both experimentation and reflection on what has been learned are important parts of the learning process;
- ○ the effective transfer of knowledge requires a strong commitment to performance improvement.

The 'double-loop learning' shown in Figure 3.17 is needed where there is greater uncertainty, less predictability and more change within the external environment.

The experience of the BPiPG has identified that the substantial changes associated with the more advanced forms of partnering demand 'double-loop learning' or even 'triple-loop learning'. These more advanced forms of learning involve questioning existing organisational norms and values and setting new priorities, which may well lead to a modification of the organisation's goals and a restructuring of its value systems. They critically examine the underpinning assumptions of current practice and create the conflict and contention deemed essential for creativity. Vital elements of this process include the open provision of information and the unlearning of previous learning, and the rethinking of learning cycles, neither of which is easy to achieve. Indeed, the ability to achieve 'double-loop' and 'triple-loop learning' is much more elusive than 'single-loop learning'. This is particularly the case in bureaucratised organisations such as RSLs and their projects, whose fundamental organising principles often operate in a way that actually obstructs the learning process. For example, the bureaucratisation of RSLs tends to create fragmented patterns of thought and action. In the past, major hierarchical and horizontal divisions have been erected which means that information and knowledge rarely flows in a free manner. Different parts of the organisations and different organisations thus often operate on the basis of different pictures of the total situation and pursue different sub-units of overall goals almost as ends in themselves. The existence of such divisions also tends to foster the development of political systems that place further boundaries in the way of learning. In this situation, employees and project participants are encouraged to occupy and keep a predefined place within the whole and, indeed, are often rewarded for doing so. In view of these substantial barriers to the deeper forms of learning the BPiPG has identified the need for external facilitation to help partners in confronting these problems and developing the ability to question, challenge, and change operating norms and assumptions.

The work of the BPiPG has also identified the need for learning upstream of RSLs in the process and downstream of the main contractor. Upstream of RSLs, the Housing Corporation and local authority officers need to increase their awareness of the general principles of partnering and how to assess the effectiveness of the partnering approaches of RSLs and their suppliers. Downstream, main contractors need to develop the knowledge of specialist and trade subcontractors to build on their strengths and address their weaknesses.

Supplier development programmes have been used to considerable effect in other industries, where they are replacing the traditional purchasing function. The idea behind this is that a cross-functional team from the customer organisation works closely with suppliers to seek improvements in the suppliers' people and processes as well as at the interfaces with the customer's processes.

Promoting learning in the supply chains

Devon and Cornwall Housing Association included an item in their project documentation to Midas Homes enabling a number of craft operatives to be trained and registered on the Construction Skills Certification Scheme.

3.28. The key actions to be taken by RSLs

These are presented as an implementation audit table.

RSL implementation audit table

Actions	By when	Specific actions required	What implementation looks like
Promote learning in your organisation and throughout your supply chains			
Ensure that the pace at which you drive change in your supply chains matches the rate of learning			
Ensure that learning in your own organisation and that of your partners remains focused on the objectives of the partnership			
Encourage your employees and partners to adopt 'double-loop' and, later, 'triple-loop learning'			
Recognise and accommodate the social, political and cultural aspects of learning			
Identify the key players involved in your supply chains and use the growing openness in your relationships to undertake an audit of their current skills, experiences and expertise, and collectively identify areas where learning and improvement are required			
Allocate a budget for the learning to support partnering in your own organisation and in your schemes and supply chains			
Use a range of strategies to support learning such as intranets, electronic links between organisations and scheme developments, extranets, continuous improvement routines and computerised documentation systems			
Network with other leading developing RSLs and leading clients in other sectors of the industry to identify best practice in the learning to support more collaborative procurement approaches and win–win thinking			
Engage with outside learning support agencies such as Rethinking Construction, the Movement for Innovation, the Housing Forum, and universities and research institutions			

3.29. The key collective actions to be taken

Actions	By when	Specific actions required	What implementation looks like
Leaders of all the partners to constantly demonstrate that they are committed to individual, intraorganisational, and collective cross-organisational learning to support partnering			
Leaders to encourage and support the shift from 'single-loop' to 'double-loop' and, later, 'triple-loop learning'			
Leaders to actively seek to remove barriers to learning such as political defensive routines			
Leaders to reward effective individual, organisational and cross-organisational learning			
Partners to contribute financially to a budget and in kind to support collective learning			
Partners to provide the learning programmes within their own organisations to prepare their people, change their culture and develop the attitudes, behaviours and skills needed for their new roles and responsibilities in the relationship			
Assign task forces, champions, steering groups, stakeholder panels, advisors and facilitators to promote the learning needed for partnering and to address the barriers to change			
Encourage and enable staff exchanges and secondments between the organisations involved in order to increase joint understanding of issues, problems, processes and ways of working			
Make the culture of training, learning and personal development part of the working day in social housing schemes			
All partners to re-skill in the 'soft' skills such as talking and listening, communication, effective meetings and workshops, teamwork, leadership and championing change, learning, developing mutual understanding, resolving conflict, addressing ambiguity and confusion, creative problem-solving, and the rationalisation and justification of decisions			
Develop skills in specific tools and techniques such as value and risk management and process mapping			
Seek accreditation for learning from professional and other bodies			
Use the services of the Construction Best Practice Programme and other agencies to support learning by, for example, attending workshops, joining Construction Best Practice Clubs and visiting companies under the auspices of Inside UK Enterprise – Construction			
Partners to develop links with universities, colleges, schools and professional institutions			
Partners to provide work experience and industrial training placements for undergraduates and technicians			

3.30. The key barriers to be addressed

Key barriers	Proposed Solutions
Ensuring top management commitment and the appropriate allocation of resources needed for such a challenging learning programme	
Addressing the industry's traditional lack of commitment to training and learning	
Achieving the level of learning needed to support new ways of thinking, acting, behaving and reacting if the main contractor and consultants and specialist and trade contractors are to operate as an integrated team	
The continuing short-term nature of relationships in many scheme developments which perpetuate the lack of commitment to collective and ongoing learning	
The lack of trust to support the honesty and openness needed for the sharing of information and knowledge between partners and to remove defensive routines and 'spin' deep within the partnering organisations	
The difficulties of shifting from 'single-loop' to 'double-loop' and, later, 'triple-loop learning'	
The lack of time to undertake the learning and knowledge transfer needed in schemed development	
The lack of experience of leaders and managers in coaching learners	
The lack of appropriately skilled and experienced external supporters and facilitators of learning	

Section 4

Overall conclusions and recommendations

4.1. The key features of the BPiPG's approach to partnering

Using the findings from its research project and from a review of other experiences of the use of the more advanced forms of partnering in construction and other sectors of the economy, the BPiPG has identified what it considers to be an appropriate RSL-led approach to partnering which fits the specificity of the social housing sector. It includes those characteristics of partnering outlined in the Housing Corporation's Scheme Development Standards, and the ECI publication *Partnering in the Social Housing Sector*. However, the view of the BPiPG is that although these place considerable emphasis on 'policy and strategy', 'the building of relationships' and 'performance measurement', there is still insufficient recognition of the wider range of other factors involved. Consequently, the BPiPG has sought to develop a more holistic and systematic approach to partnering which builds on, but also extends and deepens, previous more organic and informal approaches to partnering. It proposes a framework for change that incorporates seven key elements, all of which, we argue, need to be in place if value and mutual competitive advantage are to be added through continuous improvement.

The approach reflects the growing awareness in construction and other sectors of the economy that the more advanced forms of partnering conform to the key features of an advanced form of innovation, in that it is:

○ complex and involves a number of interrelated factors;
○ cumulative and evolutionary in that it is built on previous innovations;
○ a strategic and long-term approach requiring top management commitment and champions;
○ dependent upon effective intra- and interorganisational relationships;

○   dependent upon strong interactions with the external environment;
○   dependent on continuous and collective learning;
○   adopted and implemented in number of stages or phases.

At the heart of our approach is the need to add value for the end users and to increase mutual competitive advantage for all the parties. A clear policy and strategy is seen as being necessary in order to articulate clearly the reasons for adopting partnering, the scope of the proposed approach and the strategies for its implementation. Through internal audits and reviews of the external environment, RSLs need to identify the key areas of their business and development projects where they need to enhance their present skills, competencies and competitiveness through partnering with other organisations. This report incorporates a series of audit implementation checklists in respect of each element of the model to assist RSLs to evaluate their operation, suppliers and the market in which they operate. It also includes a series of audit implementation checklists for consultants and contractors so that they can evaluate their relationship with their partner RSLs against each of the elements of the model.

The key to the scope of an RSL-led approach to partnering is the degree of influence and leverage they have over their potential partners in persuading them to enter into the more advanced forms of partnering with their closer, more open and longer-term relationships. Having taken the decision to partner, its adoption and implementation needs to be planned thoroughly in a way which sets an appropriate pace of change for the parties involved, and which takes into account their capacity for change. The BPiPG recommends that those RSLs partnering for the first time should initially limit their new relationships to consultants and main contractors – their first-tier suppliers. RSLs need to have their leaders and champions prepared and in place to drive forward the change and to take people with them by diffusing the approach throughout their organisation. Having established what they are looking for from the proposed partnership with consultants and main contractors the RSLs can then begin the vitally important process of choosing the most appropriate partners by assessing their skills and competencies against their needs and scheme requirements. Initially the BPiPG would recommend that those RSLs new to partnering should restrict the duration of the partnering relationship to a specific pilot project but with the longer-term objective of moving to a framework or term agreement over a period of time. Having formed the most appropriate partnership, the parties can then begin the process of working together to develop the pilot scheme whilst using value management and other improvement techniques to reduce waste, and to add value for the end users and other stakeholders. A good starting point is to analyse the current processes and interactions and unpack the business-to-business relationships into all interrelated contacts between the individuals involved. In this way, both the formal and informal structures within and between the partner organisations can be revealed. Incentives can be used to encourage collaborative behaviour and reward the learning and innovation leading to improvements in product and process. The new relationships should be monitored on a regular basis to measure their effectiveness against key performance measures such as HQIs and KPIs. Such performance measures, benchmarked against previous projects, are needed to avoid complacency and to collect the evidence to justify the decision to shift from price-competitive to collaborative procurement.

4.2. The key factors in successfully implementing the approach

The BPiPG's project has confirmed a number of issues that are seen as being critical to the effective adoption and implementation of the model in its more advanced forms. Partners need to collectively agree strategic goals for the whole supply chain. Senior managers need to demonstrate strong, visible and sustained commitment and leadership. The parties have to be keen to improve and willing to work collaboratively with customers and suppliers in adopting continuous improvement and win–win thinking. Continuous improvement and problem-solving teams need to be set up and empowered to understand existing relationships and processes and develop new and better ways of working. RSLs and their first-tier suppliers need to move beyond their often very rudimentary partnering arrangements to become directly involved in the process of change and improvement within their supply chains.

Early experiences of the adoption of the partnering approach indicate that its success is closely dependent upon:

O The commitment and ability of the RSL in spearheading this new approach to shaping, managing and developing supply chains.

O The RSL having sufficient volume and continuity of development work to provide the necessary leverage over their suppliers to bring about a change of attitudes, behaviour, and ways of working needed, and to attack the rationalisation of failure and complacency that exists in much of their supply systems.

O The RSL providing strong and effective leadership in setting the direction of the change, overcoming resistance, and setting an example in developing the attitudes, and the behaviour and learning and innovation needed within and between the organisations involved.

O The RSL and its partners having a full understanding of the strategic implications of the more advanced forms of partnering and its complexity as a multifactor innovation.

O A strong belief in the win–win ethos at the heart of partnering at all levels within and between the organisations.

O A strategic and long-term commitment to more collaborative approaches by top management in the RSL and its supplier organisations.

O The creation of a creative and no-blame culture within and between the parties.

O A clear statement of policy, objectives and critical success factors from the RSL.

O A robust and transparent approach, including the most appropriate selection criteria, for selecting the right partners for long-term customer–supplier relationships.

O Careful selection of first-tier partners with compatible processes and structures, collaborative capability and with the potential for culture change and creative problem-solving, rather than just price-based selection criteria.

O The acceptance by all the partners of the need for closer and longer-term interorganisational relationships with a very much smaller number of customers and suppliers.

O The degree of preparedness of the personnel and organisations involved, particularly in relation to the 'soft' interpersonal skills, attitudes and behaviours that underpin closer and more open and trusting relationships.

○ The allocation of appropriate resources by the RSL and its partners over the considerable period of time it takes to adopt and implement partnering, and to subsequently sustain it.

○ The RSL and its first-tier suppliers developing a more inclusive approach to procurement to include specialist and trade subcontractors, suppliers and other stakeholders.

○ A more equitable sharing of risks and rewards.

○ Striking an appropriate balance between the form of contract and the type of business relationship.

○ The development of greater openness, transparency and trust so that probity and best value can be demonstrated.

○ A continuous improvement culture and methodology that includes robust measures of performance and targets for improvement.

○ Teamwork and the development of joint problem-solving capabilities.

○ A commitment to continuous and shared learning.

○ Making the appropriate types and amounts of assets specific to the partnership.

Each of the elements of the BPiPG's approach requires a considerable departure from existing ways of working, which implies a change of culture for which the people involved need to be prepared. The project has confirmed that more advanced partnering requires not only changes in the relationships between the parties involved but also attitudinal, behavioural, structural and cultural changes deep within the participating organisations. It requires the parties to break with their traditional approach to managing people and allow their staff the freedom to experiment with and develop new ways of working with their partners. It involves changing the rules of the game and challenging the prevailing orthodoxy in scheme development with regard to professional and commercial relationships between RSLs, consultants, main contractors/developers and their supply chains. This means that organisations need to view partnering as a strategic innovation that will have implications for the way in which they conduct their business. For this reason, it is vital that in its more advanced forms it is not considered to be just another procurement route.

4.3. The benefits of more collaborative relationships

Although the BPiPG's approach aims to develop new customer–supplier relationships on the basis of rational and quantitative decision-making, it is still difficult to quantify in advance the benefits of such an approach as there are still limited data on the effectiveness of partnering in the social housing sector. At the moment, therefore, it is not yet possible to spell out in advance either the exact form of the relationship or the specific measurable benefits that partnering might bring. This means that the move to partnering cannot be judged solely on the basis of quantified and clear commercial objectives and, at present, requires, to some extent, a step in the dark, requiring boldness, initiative and faith on the part of RSLs and their consultants and main contractors. The faith shown by the members of the BPiPG in embarking on their approach was based on a number of factors including the positive experiences of construction's commercial clients in other sectors of construction, the advice offered by HM Treasury, various government initiatives and reports, and the Housing Corporation's targets for Egan compliance. It was also, in part, based on an instinctive and philosophical belief by the practitioners involved that current procurement methods are not entirely satisfactory and that the new scheme development process requires new 'game rules', rules which cannot be fully written in advance but which will emerge over time.

Although the BPiPG's project was focused on the early stages of setting up a partnering approach, it did begin to demonstrate the benefits to be derived from partnering, provided it is undertaken appropriately. The main benefit to RSLs is that their first-tier suppliers are more focused on their needs, those of their tenants, the Housing Corporation and other stakeholders. Through closer relationships and more open communication, coupled with HQIs and the greater use of techniques such as value management, the consultants and main contractors are able to more clearly identify what constitutes real value for RSLs and their tenants. In the longer term, the aim is that consultants, main contractors and their supply chains can also benefit from the partnership through the greater certainty of future work and ring-fenced margins. The closer and more trusting relationships were beginning to encourage the sharing of technical and commercial information so that improvements could be made and performance more openly monitored. A more synergistic combination of both functional and cross-functional teams had begun to play an important part in identifying value, reducing waste and managing risk. For example, teamworking and earlier supplier involvement during the design stage resulted in higher HQI scores than those achieved on previous benchmark projects. Involving all the partners at the earliest possible stage in the project and encouraging them to contribute to joint value and risk management should over time help to minimise the possibility of future misunderstandings that can lead to conflict and inefficiency and waste.

Although a number of the disruptions, problems and barriers associated with the pilot projects were in the hands of the partners, a number were also attributable to external agencies and influences outside of the direct control of the partners. By working more closely and openly together, the partners were all becoming more aware of nature of these problems and disruptions and their effects. Their combined skills, knowledge and resources were increasingly being brought to bear on addressing these difficulties, and, to an extent, helping to introduce a greater degree of stability and predictability to their businesses. In this way, partnering appears not only to allow the parties to strengthen their competitive position, but also to reduce environmental uncertainty, by making the actions of customers and suppliers more predictable and transparent.

As well as assisting in identifying the key issues to be addressed in improving new scheme developments it also helps to identify the main sources of leverage, competencies and expertise within the partnership that can be brought to bear on addressing these issues. Decision-making tends to be more rational and based on greater openness and shared information, and partners become more skilful in negotiating on the basis of evidence and fact. Although this can sometimes be uncomfortable for the people involved, it often results in more innovative but practical solutions. More individual and collective learning takes place to support innovation, and there is greater motivation to find out about new technical and organisational thinking and new management approaches. This closer interchange of ideas also contributes to the development of greater openness, transparency and trust and, by increasingly reaching deep into relationships, it can help address differences before they become sources of conflict. Although from time to time mistakes are made, differences still arise, and communication breaks down, problems can be resolved in a more constructive and less adversarial way.

There was a growing understanding of the leverage needed to effect change in the supply chains, increase mutual competitive advantage, build collaboration, integrate processes and increase external and internal customer focus. The experience of the BPiPG would suggest that main contractors would require a programme of about 100 units per year to generate the influence necessary to justify changes in their ways of working and refocus their long-term investment in continuous improvement. However, very much smaller annual development programmes may be attractive to smaller local main contractors.

As a result of their greater understanding of mutual advantage and win–win thinking, and the development of more synergistic relationships, partners were beginning to feel more comfortable in contributing their managerial and/or technical expertise and knowledge to the partnership in a more open and creative way. This transfer of knowledge was becoming a valuable source of innovative ideas, as partners were increasingly required to prepare detailed explanations and justifications of operations they are familiar with and may not have examined objectively for some time. The process of putting this knowledge to the test can generate valuable new ideas. Partnering brings the parties closer together as they come to understand each other's way of doing things, and their degree of freedom and room for manoeuvre. A further benefit that arises from a well-managed partnership is that it can provide the partners with a mechanism to bring the challenge of competition to parts of their organisation that have in the past been shielded from it. This can be a real benefit if those parts of the organisation respond positively by re-examining their preconceived ideas and generating a desire to change and innovate.

4.4. The concerns associated with more collaborative approaches

The approach advocated by the BPiPG is very different from the way in which RSLs and other project participants currently conduct their business and undertake the development of schemes. This means that there are also considerable challenges to be addressed if its adoption and implementation is to be successful. The difficulties and complexities associated with gaining employee and partner commitment should not be underestimated. Although in most cases the individuals and parties rationally accept the benefits of partnering, their cultures may not be readily compatible, and its implementation may face strong resistance if they are not accompanied by closer strategic relationships and appropriate measures to internally prepare for its implementation. In addition, the BPiPG's approach to partnering is a multielement innovation. Adopting all the elements of the BPiPG's approach requires considerable intra- and interorganisational change over a broad range of issues, and the partners need to develop new ways of working which demand a new range of skills and competencies. Considerable learning is needed to raise awareness of partnering and in gaining and understanding the goals of all the parties involved. As well as the provision of advice, training and support to develop these skills, particular attention needs to be paid to the timing of decisions as well as the degree of openness and honesty required.

It needs to be recognised that adopting and implementing the BPiPG's approach to partnering is difficult and requires a great deal of commitment, careful planning, effort and resources over a long period of time. It requires openness and transparency, courage, patience and persistence, and energy from all the parties. It requires an agreed process for dealing with setbacks, barriers and problems and frustrations that inevitably arise from time to time on the way. It needs to be recognised that there are a number of steps in adopting and implementing partnering and that initial progress is often very slow as time and learning is needed to raise awareness of the many factors involved. It also takes time to build the necessary relationships, openness and transparency before moving to the reshaping of organisational and interface structures and processes. Also, there is always the danger that longer-term and closer relationships can lead to complacency unless there are stretching improvement targets alongside robust performance measurement systems.

The inability of many RSLs to provide the necessary volume and continuity of work is a major concern. Changes in relationships, processes and interface structures and product offerings will be severely constrained when the duration of the partnership is restricted to a single project. The experience of the BPiPG confirms that it is difficult for suppliers to respond in any significant way to the requirements of specific RSLs on the basis of an irregular flow of work on a project-by-project basis. Also, Section 106 sites usually offer no or very restricted opportunities to partner. It therefore needs to be recognised that the benefits from project-specific partnering are limited and that RSLs with a sufficiently large and regular new-build programme should consider ways of progressing over time to more strategic partnering within a framework or term agreement.

As progress in developing partnerships owes much to the effectiveness of relationships between individuals, the present high levels of staff turnover in the development departments of RSLs must be seen as a major barrier to building the individual relationships that are so necessary in implementing and sustaining effective partnering. It is important that the same team is used over a number of projects to increase understanding, develop trust and capture learning and carry it forward to the next project. Further inhibiting factors are the limited internal preparedness of the partners and the lack of robust historical data relating to previous performance against KPIs. The lack of standardisation of RSL specifications and their complex and prescriptive nature can also limit empowerment of suppliers and inhibit innovations to product and process in the supply chains. Overly complex specifications and documentation place too much emphasis on solutions rather than performance or value, and can preclude the use of much of the main contractors' supply chains. This means that RSLs cannot exploit the advantage of the leverage that main contractors/developers have over their suppliers.

The lack of commitment to total quality management and continuous improvement by most construction organisations can be seen as a further concern. Although the concept of continuous improvement is now more widely understood within the pilot projects the full benefits of total quality management are yet to be appreciated and realised. The lack of explicit intraorganisational measures of performance, such as those in the 'Business Excellence' model, also contribute to the difficulties of choosing the right partners and assembling the evidence to demonstrate improvements in performance. Although HQIs, and to a more limited extent KPIs, are proving to be helpful in improving performance, there has been, however, less progress in relation to the collection of data and their more imaginative presentation. This is in part explained by the simplistic nature of the national system of KPIs and that they relate to year-on-year or end-of-project assessments of performance that do not fit comfortably with the much shorter duration 'plan–do–check–act' cycle associated with continuous improvement in other industries. There is also an understandable reluctance by contractors to be open and divulge sensitive information in relation to KPIs that may affect their reputation on the basis of what could be a one-off pilot project. The adoption of continuous improvement is also limited by the length of relationships associated with project-specific partnering. RSLs need to recognise the limitations of project-specific partnering and work towards longer-term strategic partnering. Indeed, RSLs are increasingly, and with considerable success, introducing partnering in the maintenance and refurbishment of properties because there is much less external interference and the planning and funding of work is much more within their own financial planning and control.

The limited understanding of the nature of business and project processes is a further barrier to performance improvement. The lack of attention to processes and their mapping and integration means that process improvement is difficult. Without such tools it is difficult to determine 'who' does 'what', 'where', 'when', 'why' and 'how' in the process, and identify where waste occurs and where value is added. It also makes it difficult to identify and assess the impact of change in one part of the process may have on another.

A further concern is the traditional lack of individual and organisational learning in construction generally. Partnering is a substantial and challenging innovation that requires considerable 'double-loop' learning, which needs to be undertaken collectively as well as individually within the partnership. There is also a need for external support for this collective learning, but at present there is a lack of appropriate partnering guidance and advice, trainers and courses to support partners in their learning.

The project has also confirmed the upstream inhibitors to strategic partnering such as the present funding and planning regimes that introduce a high degree of uncertainty at the front end of projects. The Housing Corporation should be commended on its increasingly clear strategic commitment to partnering and its growing awareness of the possible benefits but also the risks, difficulties and barriers involved, and the time needed for its full implementation. Also, although its commitment to the policy for partnering is clear, its implementation strategies are not yet fully focused on supporting this strategic commitment to partnering. It needs to vigorously seek out and remove the barriers to this form of partnering upstream in, and external to, the process, as many of these are outside the control of or the zone of influence of individual RSLs and their first-tier suppliers. It needs to support, encourage and sustain groups of successful partners (as measured by HQIs and KPIs) by providing a more consistent stream of funding to ensure more continuous building programmes and a more regular and predictable flow of work. This will facilitate the development of longer-term relationships and the retention of teams in strategic partnerships or alliances. This should create the conditions and environment for a reshaping of supply systems, continuous improvement, greater commitment of assets and joint innovation and learning. Such an increase in the amount of funding to partnering RSLs will also give them sufficient volume of development work to provide the option of multiple sourcing, using a small number of preferred suppliers rather than accept the risks associated with single-source supply.

The Housing Corporation should look to rethinking its funding allocation processes to allow RSLs much more responsiveness in relation to development opportunities and land purchases. This could comprise, for example, the provision of a 3-year allocation to be used at their own discretion and which would give RSLs more control over their building programme and help them to generate additional leverage over their consultants, contractors and suppliers. Shifting funding from the time spans associated with individual projects to those associated with a longer period of time or number of projects would allow RSLs to enter term or framework agreements with their key suppliers. This, in turn, would enable them to exert greater pressure for change and improvement.

The strategic allocation of funding within regions would also be helpful in this respect by allowing greater flexibility in matching demand, funding and sites for development. An alternative approach would be to pass more of the land acquisition role to those main contractors who are also developers, with RSLs focusing more on the subsequent management and maintenance of schemes. However, it must be acknowledged that Section 106 sites can restrict RSLs' choice of main contractor and prevent them from channeling the work to their partners in their preferred supply chains.

The research has also identified the impact of local authorities on joint scheme development programmes involving RSLs and local authorities. Although partnerships between local authorities and RSLs are resulting in significant, long-term programmes that can be seen as supporting partnering, the process can be very bureaucratic. This has increased the significance of the role played by local authorities in either promoting or impeding the move to partnering. This means that there is a greater need for local authorities to raise their awareness of the concept of partnering and include the ability of an RSL to partner as one of the measures in drawing up their lists of preferred RSLs within their region. They should also take the effectiveness of RSLs' partnering into account when approving specific schemes and ensure that new scheme developments are directed to those partnerships that have demonstrated their effectiveness against a range of performance measures including KPIs and HQIs. Similarly, they should take the effectiveness of partnerships into account when presenting and recommending transfer options to local authority tenants.

Local authorities need to recognise their pivotal role in social housing schemes and helping to provide the volume and continuity of work needed if RSLs are to adopt the more advanced forms of partnering. For example, they need to rethink their relationships with preferred RSLs on the basis of the effectiveness of their partnering relationships rather than on the basis of geographical location. Although some local authorities have considered developing a local-authority-wide partnering contract involving all their partner RSLs, it might be better for RSLs to recognise their supply chains and work with other local authorities that a partnering RSL services.

These may be somewhat geographically remote within a region but the local authorities could look to manage their investment to support partnering groups to achieve value for money through cost savings and quality.

There are further barriers to the effectiveness of partnering to be found downstream in the process. As in most of construction there is little in the way of formalised systems of supply chain management between main contractors and specialist and trade subcontractors and suppliers. This means there is often a lack of openness and trust in the relationships and processes with specialist and trade subcontractors. If the social housing sector is to successfully embrace the changes needed to radically improve performance, specialist and trade subcontractors need to play a more significant role in performance improvement, given that they account for as much as 80% of project expenditure. Other sectors of the economy and some sectors of construction are already developing a more participative role for their key suppliers. Unlike these other industries and sectors, the social housing sector has so far done little to develop closer and more harmonious links with specialist and trade subcontractors and give them a more central role in its efforts to improve effectiveness and become more competitive. The project has also revealed the weaknesses of specialist and trade subcontractors in social housing schemes. As many of these subcontractors are small to medium enterprises (SMEs), they lack the resources and expertise to improve their performance without the support and encouragement of RSLs, consultants and main contractors.

Section 5

Recommendations for further work and investigation

Although a great deal has been achieved by the project by increasing awareness of partnering and its adoption in the social housing sector, the BPiPG's approach has yet to be fully implemented and evaluated. However, the research has identified a number of issues and areas for further investigation that were outside the scope of the current project. These include the need to:

○ Increase understanding of how to develop the relationships associated with strategic partnering and how to make the successful transition from project-specific to strategic partnering.

○ Develop cost-effective and user-friendly process and value-mapping tools that can be used in the project processes and supply systems to new scheme developments.

○ Develop more robust measures and methodologies for assessing the effectiveness of partnerships in order that public funding can be directed to supporting the most effective partnering teams.

○ Develop robust methodologies to help RSLs and their partners shift the emphasis from capital to whole-life costs.

○ Identify the learning requirements of partners and design learning programmes to develop their skills in building relationships, integrating processes and increasing customer focus.

○ Define the role of partnering advisors or facilitators.

○ Develop a programme to provide partnering advisors or facilitators with the knowledge and skills to help support RSLs and their suppliers in adopting, implementing and sustaining partnering.

○ Redefine the role of cost and design consultants at the interface between an RSL and the main contractor in the more advanced forms of partnering.

○ Redefine the role for main contractors in the more advanced forms of partnering.

○ Develop a larger pool of main contractors/developers more able to effectively respond to the new opportunities and challenges presented by partnering.

○ Produce guidance on effective supply chain management specifically aimed at main contractors and their relationships with specialist and trade subcontractors and suppliers.

○ Investigate the relationship between the Social Housing Grant and value management.

Bibliography

Barlowe, J., Cohen, M., Jashpara, A. and Simpson Y. (1997) *Towards Positive Partnering*. The Policy Press, Bristol.

Bennett, J. and Jayes, S. (1995) *Trusting the Team*. The Reading Construction Forum, Reading.

Bennett, J. and Jayes, S. (1998) *The Seven Pillars of Partnering*. The Reading Construction Forum, Reading.

Berk, J. and Berk, S. (1993) *Total Quality Management: Implementing Continuous Improvement*. Sterling Publishing, New York.

Brundtland, G. H. (1987) *Our Common Future*. UN World Commission on Environment and Development. Oxford University Press, Oxford.

Burnes, B. (2000) *Managing Change: A Strategic Approach to Organisational Dynamics*. Financial Times and Prentice-Hall, Harlow.

Chartered Institute of Building (1996) *Code of Practice for Project Management for Construction and Development*. Pearson, Edinburgh.

Christopher, M. (1998) *Logistics and Supply Chain Management: Strategies for Reducing Cost and Improving Service*, 2nd Edn. Financial Times and Prentice-Hall, London.

Christopher, M. and Juttner, U. (2000) Developing strategic partnerships in the supply chain: a practitioner perspective. *European Journal of Purchasing and Supply Management* **6**, 117–27.

CIRIA (2000) *The Handbook of Supply Chain Management: The Essentials*. CIRIA, London.

Construction Best Practice Programme (1999) *Key Performance Indicators*. DETR, London.

Cox, A. and Thompson, I. (1998) *Contracting for Business Success*. Thomas Telford, London.

Cox, A. and Townsend, M. (1998) *Strategic Procurement in Construction: Towards Better Practice in the Management of Construction Supply Chains*. Thomas Telford, London.

Department of the Environment, Transport and the Regions (1999) *Housing Quality Indicators*. DETR, London.

Dickson, T. (1997) *Mastering Management*. Financial Times and Pitman, London.

Dixon, N. M. (2000) *Common Knowledge: How Companies Thrive by Sharing What They Know*. Harvard Business, Watertown, MA.

Dobson, P. (1988) Changing culture. *Employment Gazette*, Dec., 647–50.

Easterby-Smith, M., Burgoyne, J. and Araujo, L. (1999) *Organisational Learning and the Learning Organisation: Developments in Theory and Practice*. Sage, London.

Edvinson, L. (2002) *Corporate Longitude*. Pearson, Edinburgh.

Egan, J. (1998) *Rethinking Construction*. Department of the Environment, Transport and the Regions, London.

European Construction Institute (1997) *Partnering in the Public Sector: A Toolkit*. ECI, Loughborough.

European Construction Institute (1997) *Partnering in the Social Housing Sector: A Handbook*. Thomas Telford, London.

Fairclough, J. (2002) *Rethinking Construction Innovation and Research: A Review of Government R&D Policies and Practices*. DTLR, London.

Gann, D. M. and Salter, A. J. (2000) Innovation in project-based, service enhanced firms in the construction of complex products and systems. *Research Policy* **29**, 955–72.

Gray, C. (1996) *Value for Money: Helping the UK Afford the Buildings it Likes*. Thomas Telford, London.

Hines, P. (1994) *Creating World-class Suppliers: Unlocking Mutual Competitive Advantage*. Financial Times and Pitman, London.

Hines, P. and Taylor, D. (2000) *Going Lean: A Guide to Implementation*. Lean Enterprise Research Centre, Cardiff Business School, Cardiff.

HM Treasury (1997) *Government Construction Procurement Guidance*, Guidance No. 1. *Essential Requirements for Construction Procurement Guide*. Office of Government Commerce, London.

HM Treasury (1997) *Government Construction Procurement Guidance*, Guidance No. 2. *Value for Money in Construction Procurement*. Office of Government Commerce, London.

HM Treasury (1997) *Government Construction Procurement Guidance*, Guidance No. 3. *Appointment of Consultants and Contractors*. Office of Government Commerce, London.

HM Treasury (1997) *Government Construction Procurement Guidance*, Guidance No. 4. *Teamworking, Partnering and Incentives*. Office of Government Commerce, London.

HM Treasury (1997) *Government Construction Procurement Guidance*, Guidance No. 5. *Procurement Strategies*. Office of Government Commerce, London.

HM Treasury (1997) *Government Construction Procurement Guidance*, Guidance No. 6. *Financial Aspects of Projects*. Office of Government Commerce, London.

HM Treasury (1997) *Government Construction Procurement Guidance*, Guidance No. 7. *Whole Life Costs*. Office of Government Commerce, London.

HM Treasury (1997) *Government Construction Procurement Guidance*, Guidance No. 8. *Project Evaluation and Feedback*. Office of Government Commerce, London.

HM Treasury (1997) *Government Construction Procurement Guidance*, Guidance No. 9. *Benchmarking*. Office of Government Commerce, London.

HM Treasury (1997) *Government Construction Procurement Guidance*, Guidance No. 10. *Achieving Excellence through Health and Safety*. Office of Government Commerce, London.

Holti, R., Nicolini, D. and Smalley, M. (2000) *The Handbook of Supply Chain Management*. CIRIA, London.

Housing Corporation (2000) *Scheme Development Standards*. Housing Corporation, London.

Industrial Society (1997) *Culture Change. Managing Best Practice 35*. Industrial Society, London.

Jones, M. and Saad, M. (1998) *Unlocking Specialist Potential. A More Participative Role for Specialist Contractors*. Reading Construction Forum. Thomas Telford, London.

Lamming, R. (1993) *Beyond Partnership: Strategies for Innovation and Lean Supply*. Prentice-Hall, New York.

Lascelles, D. and Peacock, R. (1996) *Self-assessment for Business Excellence*. McGraw-Hill, London.

Latham, M. (1994) *Constructing the Team*. HMSO, London.

Luffman, G., Lea, E., Sanderson, S. and Kenny, B. (2000) *Strategic Management: An Analytical Introduction*. Blackwell, Oxford.

National Housing Federation (2002) *Implementing the Clients' Charter: A Step-by-step Guide*. National Housing Federation, London.

Probst, G. and Buchell, B. (1997) *Organisational Learning: The Competitive Advantage of the Future*. Prentice-Hall, London.

Robson, C. (2002) *Real World Research: A Resource for Social Scientists and Practitioner-researchers*, 2nd Edn. Blackwell, Oxford.

Saad, M. and Jones, M. (2001) The role of main contractors in developing customer focus up and down construction's supply chain. *In*: Erridge, A., Fee, R. and McIlroy, J. (eds) *Best Practice Procurement: Public and Private Sector Perspectives*. Gower, Aldershot.

Strategic Forum for Construction (2002) *Accelerating Change: A Report by the Strategic Forum for Construction Chaired by Sir John Egan*. Strategic Forum for Construction, London.

Tidd, J., Bessant, J. and Pavitt, K. (1997) *Managing Innovation: Integrating Technological, Market and Organisational Change*. Wiley, Chichester.

Womack, J. P. and Jones, D. T. (1996) *Lean Thinking: Banish Waste and Create Wealth in Your Corporation*. Simon and Schuster, New York.

Websites

Commission for Architecture and the Built Environment: www.cabe.org.uk
Confederation of Construction Clients: www.clientsuccess.org.uk
Construction Best Practice Programme: www.cbpp.org.uk
Construction Industry Council: www.cic.org.uk
Construction Industry Training Board: www.citb.org.uk
Construction Research and Innovation Strategy Panel: www.crisp-uk.org.uk
Department of Trade and Industry (Construction pages): www.dti.gov.uk
Design Quality Indicators: www.dqi.org.uk

Health and Safety Executive: www.hse.gov.uk
Housing Corporation: www.housingcorp.gov.uk
Housing Forum: www.thehousingforum.org.uk
Local Government Task Force: www.lgtf.org.uk
Movement for Innovation: www.m4i.org.uk
Office of Government Commerce: www.ogc.gov.uk
Rethinking Construction: www.rethinkingconstruction.org